DRUG ABUSE

OPPOSING VIEWPOINTS®

Other Books of Related Interest

DRUG ABUSE

OPPOSING VIEWPOINTS®

Tamara L. Roleff, *Book Editor*

Bruce Glassman, *Vice President*
Bonnie Szumski, *Publisher*
Helen Cothran, *Managing Editor*

OPPOSING
VIEWPOINTS®
SERIES

GREENHAVEN PRESS
An imprint of Thomson Gale, a part of The Thomson Corporation

THOMSON
━━━★━━━
GALE

Detroit • New York • San Francisco • San Diego • New Haven, Conn.
Waterville, Maine • London • Munich

LIBRARY OF CONGRESS CATALOGING-IN-PUBLICATION DATA

Drug abuse : opposing viewpoints / Tamara L. Roleff, book editor.
    p. cm. — (Opposing viewpoints series)
Includes bibliographical references and index.
ISBN 0-7377-2226-6 (lib. : alk. paper) — ISBN 0-7377-2227-4 (pbk. : alk. paper)
    1. Drug abuse. 2. Drug abuse—Prevention. 3. Narcotics, control of. 4. Drug testing. I. Roleff, Tamara L., 1959– . II. Opposing viewpoints series (Unnumbered)
HV5801.D7236 2005
362.29—dc22
                                                        2004042406

Printed in the United States of America

"Congress shall make
no law. . . abridging the
freedom of speech, or of
the press."

First Amendment to the U.S. Constitution

The basic foundation of our democracy is the First
Amendment guarantee of freedom of expression.
The Opposing Viewpoints Series is dedicated to the
concept of this basic freedom and the idea that it is
more important to practice it than to enshrine it.

Contents

Why Consider Opposing Viewpoints?

"The only way in which a human being can make some approach to knowing the whole of a subject is by hearing what can be said about it by persons of every variety of opinion and studying all modes in which it can be looked at by every character of mind. No wise man ever acquired his wisdom in any mode but this."

John Stuart Mill

In our media-intensive culture it is not difficult to find differing opinions. Thousands of newspapers and magazines and dozens of radio and television talk shows resound with differing points of view. The difficulty lies in deciding which opinion to agree with and which "experts" seem the most credible. The more inundated we become with differing opinions and claims, the more essential it is to hone critical reading and thinking skills to evaluate these ideas. Opposing Viewpoints books address this problem directly by presenting stimulating debates that can be used to enhance and teach these skills. The varied opinions contained in each book examine many different aspects of a single issue. While examining these conveniently edited opposing views, readers can develop critical thinking skills such as the ability to compare and contrast authors' credibility, facts, argumentation styles, use of persuasive techniques, and other stylistic tools. In short, the Opposing Viewpoints Series is an ideal way to attain the higher-level thinking and reading skills so essential in a culture of diverse and contradictory opinions.

In addition to providing a tool for critical thinking, Opposing Viewpoints books challenge readers to question their own strongly held opinions and assumptions. Most people form their opinions on the basis of upbringing, peer pressure, and personal, cultural, or professional bias. By reading carefully balanced opposing views, readers must directly confront new ideas as well as the opinions of those with whom they disagree. This is not to simplistically argue that everyone who reads opposing views will—or should—change his or her opinion. Instead, the series enhances readers' understanding of their own views by encouraging confrontation with opposing ideas. Careful examination of others' views can lead to the readers' understanding of the logical inconsistencies in their own opinions, perspective on why they hold an opinion, and the consideration of the possibility that their opinion requires further evaluation.

Evaluating Other Opinions

To ensure that this type of examination occurs, Opposing Viewpoints books present all types of opinions. Prominent spokespeople on different sides of each issue as well as well-known professionals from many disciplines challenge the reader. An additional goal of the series is to provide a forum for other, less known, or even unpopular viewpoints. The opinion of an ordinary person who has had to make the decision to cut off life support from a terminally ill relative, for example, may be just as valuable and provide just as much insight as a medical ethicist's professional opinion. The editors have two additional purposes in including these less known views. One, the editors encourage readers to respect others' opinions—even when not enhanced by professional credibility. It is only by reading or listening to and objectively evaluating others' ideas that one can determine whether they are worthy of consideration. Two, the inclusion of such viewpoints encourages the important critical thinking skill of objectively evaluating an author's credentials and bias. This evaluation will illuminate an author's reasons for taking a particular stance on an issue and will aid in readers' evaluation of the author's ideas.

It is our hope that these books will give readers a deeper understanding of the issues debated and an appreciation of the complexity of even seemingly simple issues when good and honest people disagree. This awareness is particularly important in a democratic society such as ours in which people enter into public debate to determine the common good. Those with whom one disagrees should not be regarded as enemies but rather as people whose views deserve careful examination and may shed light on one's own.

Thomas Jefferson once said that "difference of opinion leads to inquiry, and inquiry to truth." Jefferson, a broadly educated man, argued that "if a nation expects to be ignorant and free . . . it expects what never was and never will be." As individuals and as a nation, it is imperative that we consider the opinions of others and examine them with skill and discernment. The Opposing Viewpoints Series is intended to help readers achieve this goal.

David L. Bender and Bruno Leone,
Founders

Greenhaven Press anthologies primarily consist of previously published material taken from a variety of sources, including periodicals, books, scholarly journals, newspapers, government documents, and position papers from private and public organizations. These original sources are often edited for length and to ensure their accessibility for a young adult audience. The anthology editors also change the original titles of these works in order to clearly present the main thesis of each viewpoint and to explicitly indicate the opinion presented in the viewpoint. These alterations are made in consideration of both the reading and comprehension levels of a young adult audience. Every effort is made to ensure that Greenhaven Press accurately reflects the original intent of the authors included in this anthology.

Introduction

> *"Under federal law there is no distinction between Oxycontin . . . and drugs like cocaine, methadone, and opiates. All are Schedule II drugs, which have medical uses but a high potential for abuse, and simple possession of any of them is punishable by up to a year's imprisonment."*
>
> —*Hendrick Hertzberg*, New Yorker, *October 27, 2003*

Millions of Americans found it ironic when conservative talk show host Rush Limbaugh—who often railed against drug users, addicts, and treatment programs on his show—admitted in October 2003 that he was addicted to the prescription painkiller OxyContin. Limbaugh said he started taking the pills to alleviate the pain from his two herniated disks. Allegations later arose that Limbaugh went "doctor shopping"—visiting several physicians to get prescriptions for OxyContin without telling them about the other doctors and prescriptions. Limbaugh is also alleged to have used his former maid, Wilma Cline, as his OxyContin supplier. Cline told the *National Enquirer* and Florida police that between 1998 and 2002 she sold her employer thousands of pain pills that had been prescribed for her husband's back pain.

Introduced in 1996, OxyContin proved to be a wonder drug for patients who suffered from chronic, debilitating pain. Unlike other painkillers, whose effects last only two to four hours, OxyContin's pain relief lasts twelve hours due to the pill's unique coating that slowly releases the drug into the patient's bloodstream. It was not long, however, before drug abusers discovered that if they chewed the pill, or pulverized it and then snorted or injected the powder, they would get an immediate high that lasted hours longer than a high from other drugs such as heroin. OxyContin became a very popular drug in rural areas of the country where street drugs were not easily available, thus earning the nickname "hillbilly heroin."

The media began reporting on OxyContin abuse in 2001

with a story in *Time* magazine in which various local officials call OxyContin abuse an "epidemic" and responsible for causing a "blizzard of a crime wave" in their small towns. One official with the Drug Enforcement Administration says OxyContin is "one of the most abused prescription drugs. It's certainly the most dangerous." According to the DEA, OxyContin abuse is the fastest growing epidemic in the United States; the agency reports that 454 people died from abusing OxyContin in 2000 and 2001. Nearly 11,000 people visited hospital emergency rooms due to OxyContin abuse, three times the number of visits in 1996, when the drug was first introduced.

But for physicians who specialize in alleviating pain, the focus on OxyContin abuse has them dismayed. When some doctors heard the miraculous reports of OxyContin's effects on pain, they finally started to overcome their fear of turning their patients into addicts with a prescription of strong painkillers that had to be taken every few hours. Many began prescribing OxyContin with confidence. News stories depicting OxyContin as "hillbilly heroin," however, have made them reluctant to prescribe strong painkillers once again. In addition, the DEA announced it is "cracking down" on physicians who write too many prescriptions for the drug. Doctors who, in the DEA's opinion, overprescribe OxyContin may have their medical licenses suspended.

Some believe that the media has exaggerated the problem of OxyContin abuse. Reporter Sandeep Kaushik writes that the barrage of media stories about OxyContin—which tells addicts about the new drug, where to get it, and how to use it—"may be contributing to the increase in OxyContin abuse." He also charges that none of the sensationalistic stories about OxyContin abuse "bothered to ask how solid the numbers were" about addicts, overdoses, and related deaths. Kaushik contends that most of those whose deaths were described as being due to an OxyContin overdose actually had several other drugs in their systems that could have been responsible for their deaths. Kaushik asserts that OxyContin abuse increases in areas after stories appear in the news media, not before.

As Limbaugh's story shows, illicit drugs such as marijuana,

heroin, cocaine, and Ecstasy are not the only drugs that can be abused. Over-the-counter and prescription medications can also be misused. Prescription drug abuse—taking larger doses than prescribed, taking medications prescribed for someone else or without a doctor's prescription, or taking medications for reasons other than for which they are prescribed—is a growing problem in the United States. Most people take their prescription medications as prescribed, but the 2001 National Household Survey on Drug Abuse reports that nearly 36 million Americans between the ages of twelve and twenty-five reported misusing prescription drugs at least once in their lifetimes. According to the survey, in 2000 approximately 2 million Americans misused pain relievers for the first time; first-time stimulant abusers were about 1 million strong in 2000, while first-time users of stimulants numbered about 700,000. The number of people misusing sedatives remains relatively low—175,000 in 2000.

Many Americans believe that Limbaugh's drug problem is different from drug abuse by addicts on the street because he was addicted to a prescription drug as opposed to an illegal drug such as heroin. Indeed prescription drug addicts do not suffer the stigma faced by addicts who use illegal drugs. Sean Hannity, who hosts a show on Fox TV, believes there is a "difference between somebody who, as part of a medical treatment, had these things prescribed and it got out of hand over time, and somebody who is using drugs recreationally." Atlanta-based radio host Neal Boortz agrees: "The addiction happened while [Limbaugh] was under a legal regimen of these drugs. That is not at all the way people get addicted to heroin."

As seen by the controversy over OxyContin, the issue of drug abuse and addiction is not limited to street drugs. In *Drug Abuse: Opposing Viewpoints*, the authors debate what drugs are most abused and discuss ways to reduce such abuse in the following chapters: Are Illicit Drugs Harmful? What Causes Drug Abuse and Addiction? Should Drug Testing Be Used? How Can Drug Abuse Be Reduced? As the case of Rush Limbaugh illustrates, if a substance—legal or illegal—can be misused, people will inevitably misuse it, keeping the debates concerning drug abuse alive.

CHAPTER 1

Are Illicit Drugs Harmful?

Chapter Preface

Ideas about the harmfulness of certain drugs have changed throughout history. Indeed, many drugs that are now illegal were once legally prescribed by doctors. Opium and similar drugs, for example, have been used medicinally for thousands of years by the ancient Greeks, Egyptians, and Chinese. In Europe laudanum was a very popular over-the-counter opiate drug during the eighteenth and nineteenth centuries. Morphine, derived from opium, appeared at the turn of the nineteenth century and was called a wonder drug for its ability to mask severe pain during surgery and afterward. Heroin was also proclaimed to be a miracle drug. Its pain relief properties are even more effective than morphine or codeine. Heroin and morphine drug kits, containing a syringe and vial of the drug, were legally sold over the counter in general stores until the early 1900s when international treaties began regulating the production, distribution, and sale of opium and opium-derived drugs.

Cocaine—an extract from coca leaves—was a popular stimulant during the 1850s. Inventor Thomas Edison and actress Sarah Bernhardt were fans of the drug. The psychoanalyst Sigmund Freud promoted the use of cocaine to cure depression and impotence. Until the early 1900s, cocaine was an ingredient in the soft drink Coca-Cola, which was originally sold as "a valuable brain tonic and cure for all nervous afflictions." Cocaine was made illegal in 1920 when Congress passed the Dangerous Drug Act.

Another illegal drug that was once sold legally is LSD. LSD (lysergic acid diethylamide), a hallucinogen, was synthesized in 1938, but its mind-altering properties were not realized until the 1940s. Early research found that very small quantities of the drug produced changes in the user's behavior, perceptions, and emotions. Psychiatrists theorized that mental illnesses might be caused by biochemical imbalances in the brain that perhaps could be rectified by this new psychedelic (mind-opening) drug. LSD was used by psychiatrists to treat mental illnesses of all kinds, but especially schizophrenia. It was also deemed successful in treating alcoholics, drug addicts addicted to narcotics, psychopaths and sociopaths, and sexual deviants. Many medical patients who were near death found that LSD treatments eased their fear of dying. Most psychoanalysts and psychiatrists discontinued the use of LSD in the 1960s due to the unpredictability of the drug's effects on users.

Opium, morphine, heroin, cocaine, and LSD are all examples of drugs that were once legal and believed to be safe. Subsequent research has revealed that these drugs can be extremely addictive; however, researchers continue to disagree about their dangerousness. The authors in the following chapter examine whether other illicit drugs are harmful or can be used safely.

> "Marijuana directly affects the brain. . . . It impairs the ability of young people to concentrate and retain information during their peak learning years."

Marijuana Is Harmful

John P. Walters

John P. Walters is the director of the Office of National Drug Control Policy. In the following viewpoint Walters argues that marijuana is a potent, addictive drug that impairs brain function in teens and young adults. In addition, he asserts that attempts to legalize marijuana for medicinal purposes are based on pseudoscience and open up legal loopholes that allow dangerous drug dealers to control their cities with a reign of terror.

As you read, consider the following questions:

1. How much more potent is marijuana in 2002 than it was a generation ago, according to Walters?
2. What percentage of Americans needing drug treatment are dependent on marijuana, according to the Department of Health and Human Services?
3. What is the science about marijuana clear on, according to the author?

John P. Walters, "The Myth of Harmless Marijuana," *Washington Post*, May 1, 2002, p. A25. Copyright © 2002 by the Washington Post Book World Service/ Washington Post Writers Group. Reproduced by permission of the author.

[In December 2001] the University of Michigan released its annual survey "Monitoring the Future," which measures drug use among American youth. Very little had changed from the previous year's report; most indicators were flat. The report generated little in the way of public comment.

Yet what it brought to light was deeply disturbing. Drug use among our nation's teens remains stable, but at near-record levels, with some 49 percent of high school seniors experimenting with marijuana at least once prior to graduation—and 22 percent smoking marijuana at least once a month.

Far from Harmless

After years of giggling at quaintly outdated marijuana scare stories like the 1936 movie *Reefer Madness*, we've become almost conditioned to think that any warnings about the true dangers of marijuana are overblown. But marijuana is far from "harmless"—it is pernicious. Parents are often unaware that today's marijuana is different from that of a generation ago, with potency levels 10 to 20 times stronger than the marijuana with which they were familiar.

Marijuana directly affects the brain. Researchers have learned that it impairs the ability of young people to concentrate and retain information during their peak learning years, and when their brains are still developing. The THC [which is the active ingredient that produces the high] in marijuana attaches itself to receptors in the hippocampal region of the brain, weakening short-term memory and interfering with the mechanisms that form long-term memory. Do our struggling schools really need another obstacle to student achievement?

Marijuana smoking can hurt more than just grades. According to the Department of Health and Human Services [HHS], every year more than 2,500 admissions to the District of Columbia's overtaxed emergency rooms—some 300 of them for patients under age 18—are linked to marijuana smoking, and the number of marijuana-related emergencies is growing. Each year, for example, marijuana use is linked to tens of thousands of serious traffic accidents.

What Are Some Consequences of Marijuana Use?

- May cause frequent respiratory infections, impaired memory and learning, increased heart rate, anxiety, panic attacks, tolerance, and physical dependence.

- Use of marijuana during the first month of breast-feeding can impair infant motor development.

- Chronic smokers may have many of the same respiratory problems as tobacco smokers including daily cough and phlegm, chronic bronchitis symptoms, frequent chest colds; chronic abuse can also lead to abnormal functioning of lung tissues.

- A study of college students has shown that skills related to attention, memory, and learning are impaired among people who use marijuana heavily, even after discontinuing its use for at least 24 hours.

U.S. Drug Enforcement Administration, "Marijuana," 2002.

Research has now established that marijuana is in fact addictive. Of the 4.3 million Americans who meet the diagnostic criteria for needing drug treatment (criteria developed by the American Psychiatric Association, not police departments or prosecutors) two-thirds are dependent on marijuana, according to HHS. These are not occasional pot smokers but people with real problems directly traceable to their use of marijuana, including significant health problems, emotional problems and difficulty in cutting down on use. Sixty percent of teens in drug treatment have a primary marijuana diagnosis.

"Medical" Marijuana

Despite this and other strong scientific evidence of marijuana's destructive effects, a cynical campaign is underway, in the District and elsewhere, to proclaim the virtues of "medical" marijuana. By now most Americans realize that the push to "normalize" marijuana for medical use is part of the drug legalization agenda. Its chief funders, George Soros, John Sperling and Peter Lewis, have spent millions to help pay for referendums and ballot initiatives in states from Alaska to Maine. Now it appears that a medical marijuana campaign may be on the horizon for the District.

Why? Is the American health care system—the most sophisticated in the world—really being hobbled by a lack of smoked medicines? The University of California's Center for Medicinal Cannabis Research is currently conducting scientific studies to determine the efficacy of marijuana in treating various ailments. Until that research is concluded, however, most of what the public hears from marijuana activists is little more than a compilation of anecdotes. Many questions remain unanswered, but the science is clear on a few things. Example: Marijuana contains hundreds of carcinogens.

Moreover, anti-smoking efforts aimed at youth have been remarkably effective by building on a campaign to erode the social acceptability of tobacco. Should we undermine those efforts by promoting smoked marijuana as though it were a medicine?

While medical marijuana initiatives are based on pseudoscience, their effects on the criminal justice system are anything but imaginary. By opening up legal loopholes, existing medical marijuana laws have caused police and prosecutors to stay away from marijuana prosecutions.

Dangerous Criminals

Giving marijuana dealers a free pass is a terrible idea. In fact, thanks in part to excellent reporting in the [*Washington*] *Post*, District residents are increasingly aware that marijuana dealers are dangerous criminals. The life-without-parole convictions of leaders of Washington's K Street Crew [in 2002] are only the latest evidence of this.

As reported in the *Post* the K Street Crew was a vicious group of marijuana dealers whose decade-long reign of terror was brought to an end [in 2002] after a massive prosecution effort by Michael Volkov, chief gang prosecutor for the U.S. attorney's office. The K Street Crew is credited with at least 17 murders, including systematic killings of potential witnesses. (It should not be confused with the L Street Crew, a D.C. marijuana gang that killed eight people in the course of doing business.)

Says prosecutor Volkov: "The experience in D.C. shows that marijuana dealers are no less violent than cocaine and heroin traffickers. They have just as much money to lose, just as much turf to lose, and just as many reasons to kill as any drug trafficker."

Skeptics will charge that this kind of violence is just one more reason to legalize marijuana. A review of the nation's history with drug use suggests otherwise: When marijuana is inexpensive, as it would be if legal, use soars—bad news for the District's schools, streets and emergency rooms.

> *"Experts . . . are hard-pressed to find anyone who has died of a marijuana overdose."*

The Harmful Effects of Marijuana Use Are Exaggerated

Clarence Page

Clarence Page is a syndicated columnist for the *Chicago Tribune*. In the following viewpoint Page argues that marijuana is no more dangerous than tobacco, alcohol, and prescription drugs, all of which are legal. In fact, he asserts, it may be even less dangerous since no one has ever died from a marijuana overdose. In addition, marijuana can relieve the pain and nausea suffered by many ill patients, he asserts, so doctors should be allowed to prescribe it. Page concludes that legalizing marijuana would also put an end to lawless and violent street gangs.

As you read, consider the following questions:
1. How much more potent is marijuana in 2002 than it was a generation ago, according to a study cited by Page?
2. In the author's opinion, what are some of the illnesses that could be treated by the medical use of marijuana?
3. Which government agency confirmed the effectiveness of marijuana in treating pain, nausea, and anorexia?

O ur nation's drug czar is annoyed. If proponents have their way, the District of Columbia will vote [in 2002] to legalize marijuana for medicinal purposes for the second time. [The U.S. Court of Appeals blocked the initiative from appearing on the ballot.]

Taking Potshots at Marijuana

John P. Walters, director of the Office of National Drug Control Policy, took some potshots at the issue in a *Washington Post* piece that has been reprinted across the country. Unfortunately, he brings more smoke than light.

"After years of giggling at quaintly outdated marijuana scare stories like the 1936 movie *Reefer Madness*," he writes, "we've become almost conditioned to think that any warning about the true dangers of marijuana are overblown." He then proceeds with unintended irony to give an overblown warning of his own about "The Myth of Harmless Marijuana." He warns Baby-Boomer parents that "today's marijuana is different from that of a generation ago, with potency levels 10 to 20 times stronger than the marijuana with which they were familiar."

He doesn't say where he gets that whopper and that's too bad, since it conflicts with a federally funded investigation of marijuana samples confiscated by law enforcement over the past two decades.

Published in the January 2000 *Journal of Forensic Science*, that study found the THC content (that's the active ingredient that gets you high) had only doubled to 4.2 percent from about 2 percent from 1980 to 1997. Those are not undesirable potency levels when you are using it to relieve illness. Thousands of patients suffering from HIV, glaucoma, chemotherapy, migraines, multiple sclerosis or other similarly painful or nauseating conditions could benefit from legalized marijuana use, according to the Washington-based Marijuana Policy Project. Yes, marijuana is dangerous. So are cigarettes, liquor and prescription drugs. The question that Walters fails to address is why marijuana should be treated differently from the drugs mentioned above?

We allow adults to buy cigarettes and alcohol, even though both are highly addictive and kill thousands every year. Experts may disagree, depending on definitions, over whether marijuana smoke is "addictive" or merely "habit-forming" but both sides are hard-pressed to find anyone who has died of a marijuana overdose.

Doctors treat the ill with numerous prescription drugs that are more dangerous and addictive than marijuana. But physicians are not allowed to treat the ill with marijuana. Instead, thousands of Americans unnecessarily have become criminals by purchasing marijuana for their ill loved ones rather than see them suffer.

Luckovich. © 2000 by Creators Syndicate. Reproduced by permission.

Yet Walters lambastes what he calls the "cynical campaign under way" in the District of Columbia and elsewhere "to proclaim the virtues of medical marijuana." In fact, those "cynical" campaigners include the American Public Health Association, the *New England Journal of Medicine* and almost 80 other state and national health-care organizations that support legalizing patient access to marijuana for medicinal treatment. So far, eight states have legalized medical use of marijuana by ballot initiative or legislation. District of

Columbia voters also passed a referendum in 1998, but it has been blocked by Congress.

Where referendums have been held, they have passed. But, alas, Walters dismisses those initiatives as "based on pseudoscience." Maybe he did not read the 1999 report by the Institute of Medicine, a branch of the National Academy of Sciences. It confirmed the effectiveness of marijuana's active components in treating pain, nausea and the anorexic-wasting syndrome associated with AIDS. Walters says we should wait for more information. He praises a study now under way at the University of California's Center for Medicinal Cannabis Research. But if that study doesn't come out his way either, you have to wonder, will he ignore that one, too?

"By now most Americans realize that the push to normalize marijuana for medical use is part of the drug legalization agenda," Walters says, mentioning financier George Soros and others who have contributed to the legalization cause. Walters does not mention the billions of tax dollars that he, as drug czar, has at his disposal to push marijuana myths—with our tax money!

Another Good Reason

Instead, he arouses our passions by recounting the lawlessness of violent marijuana-dealing street gangs in the district. If anything, pot gangs offer us another good reason to legalize marijuana. After all, when a drug is outlawed, only outlaws will have the drug.

> "People who overdose sometimes die of
> runaway hyperthermia (raised body
> temperature) and tachycardia (accelerated
> heart rate)."

Ecstasy Is Harmful

Frederick V. Malmstrom

Ecstasy is an amphetamine that produces feelings of euphoria and camaraderie and mild hallucinations. In the following viewpoint Frederick V. Malmstrom argues that despite
its reputation as a "love drug," Ecstasy is a dangerous stimulant that can produce damaging side effects and can even be
fatal to abusers. Malmstrom, a retired lieutenant colonel in
the air force, is a visiting Scholar for Honor at the U.S. Air
Force Academy and a psychologist for the Ohio state prisons
in Chillicothe.

As you read, consider the following questions:
1. How many tablets of Ecstasy are smuggled into the
   United States every day, according to the *New York
   Times*?
2. What are some of the medical uses of amphetamines,
   according to Malmstrom?
3. List five of the long-term effects of Ecstasy, as cited by
   the author.

Frederick V. Malmstrom, "Ecstasy Abuse: The Danger of Getting High Without
Flying," *Flying Safety*, vol. 58, March 2002, p. 10.

When I began researching the topic of a street drug named "Ecstasy," my first reaction was, "Omigawd, not *another* one!" In ten years of experience as a clinical psychologist in the prison system, I saw there is practically nothing that people won't stuff into any orifice, bathe in or shoot up their veins in the endless quest to get high. I once had a patient who mainlined peanut butter and subsequently lost three fingers to gangrene.

Ecstasy Is Now a Culture

Yet, this Ecstasy is no ordinary street drug—it's a culture. It deserves special mention, if only for the reason that both the [U.S. Military Academy] USMA and [U.S. Air Force Academy] USAFA have recently—and sadly—found it necessary to court-martial, dismiss from service and sentence to Leavenworth, several cadets who were abusing this drug. Yes, our armed forces mean business when it comes to drug abusers.

I was surprised to find that the most popular variant of Ecstasy (3,4 methyl-enedioxymethamphetamine, or simply MDMA if you ever have a need to know) was first synthesized and patented in Germany as an appetite suppressant as early as 1912. However, it wasn't until 1 July 1985 that the Drug Enforcement Administration declared MDMA a Schedule 1 Controlled Substance. That's a roundabout way of saying in the U.S.A. Ecstasy is *illegal*.

How Out of Control Is Ecstasy?

The *New York Times* reports that around one million tablets are smuggled into the U.S. every day. Illegal use of Ecstasy has skyrocketed since the early 1990s, and the armed forces aren't immune from having their share of illegal abusers. Ecstasy is an amphetamine, with sister drugs like MDE ("Eve"), MDA ("Love"), PMA ("Death"), MDEA and MBMB. These are all popularly known as "Rave drugs" or "club drugs" because they are frequently gobbled in mass quantities at all-night parties or "Raves." A moderate 75–150 milligram pill dose is reputed to give the user a high lasting from one to three hours. MDMA is definitely the "young man's drug of choice."

For the past 10 years or so there's been a popular but unfounded belief by the lay public that these Rave drugs are relatively harmless and only promote feelings of euphoria, social closeness and mild LSD-like hallucinations. Is this so? Have we *finally* found that wonder pill which promotes only peace and harmony? If that were truly the case, then we could do away with our armed forces. . . .

I'm downright suspicious of that claim, if only because my long-term personal knowledge of drug abusers says that any kind of amphetamine is bad news. Amphetamines always have their subsequent letdown period. *I've had patients who took as long as two years to recover from their amphetamine abuse.*

Amphetamines are all "designer" drugs, a trendy way of saying the molecule doesn't exist in nature—it's created in the laboratory. Hence, since the body has no natural defenses against these molecules, there are bound to be major and unknown side effects. Indeed, my MEDLINE search of over 1200 journal articles states over and over that the long-term effects of Ecstasy abuse are just beginning to be seen.

Despite that advisory, quite a bit is known about Ecstasy's *short-term* effects—on animals. Rats and monkeys on MDMA have been known to behave impulsively, ignore danger, experience spontaneous ejaculation and prefer huddling together (social closeness?) more frequently. These are certainly ingredients guaranteed to get a human party launched quickly.

But amphetamines do have narrow medical uses, and in exceptional circumstances amphetamines have been prescribed to members of the armed forces. In 1942, Commander Joe Rochefort, USN [U.S. Navy], was prescribed amphetamines for several weeks while he was busy breaking the Japanese Navy General Operational Code, JN25b. And during the 1990 Gulf War some Coalition aircrews were prescribed carefully monitored doses of amphetamine to bolster their alertness and extend their duty days. Even so, most pilots politely declined this offer.

What Does Ecstasy Do to the Body?

Like all stimulants, MDMA cranks up the body's idle speed. That's why people who overdose sometimes die of runaway hyperthermia (raised body temperature) and tachycardia (accelerated heart rate). Like all amphetamines, MDMA gives the typical "Weekend High" followed by the "Midweek Letdown." I've listed in [the following] table some of the known effects of human MDMA abuse.

Effects of MDMA ("Ecstasy")

Immediate Effects of MDMA ("Ecstasy")
- Euphoria or joy
- Feelings of closeness and camaraderie
- Increased sexual arousal
- Hyperthermia (raised core body temperature)
- Impulsivity
- Bizarre and risky behavior
- Mild but pleasant hallucinations
- Increased reaction time
- Elevated blood pressure

Short-Term Withdrawal Effects from MDMA ("Ecstasy")
- Depression
- Paranoia and unfounded suspicion
- Ataxia (inability to control fine motor movements); clumsiness
- Anxiety
- Hostility and unsociability
- Diaphoresis (uncontrolled sweating)
- Flashbacks
- Disrupted sleep patterns

Long-Term Effects of MDMA ("Ecstasy")
- Addiction
- Brain edema (swelling)
- Hepatic (liver) damage
- Permanently decreased verbal IQ
- Brain lesions (scarring)
- Parkinsonian-symptoms (the Shakes)
- Tachycardia (irregular heart beat)
- Convulsive seizures

Annually, there are about a dozen deaths in the U.S. attributed solely to Ecstasy chemical overdose. In addition, there are perhaps three yearly deaths per 10,000 in the 18–25 age group, persons who die because of behavior changes while under the influence. I found a few reported cases of exceptional bonehead abusers. One was killed while "automobile surfing" (use your imagination!) and yet another elected to climb a high-voltage tower (Famous Last Words: "Hey fellas, watch me!").

MDMA Abuse Is Easily Detected

In the short run, our medics can easily test for MDMA abuse with a simple urine or blood test. More tellingly, examiners can also determine anyone's history of MDMA abuse with hair sample analysis. Hair sample analysis is quite sensitive, dipping down into the nanogram per milligram ranges. Merely going "cold turkey" won't disguise past evidence of Ecstasy abuse.

This Stuff Is Downright Dangerous

I was disappointed to learn there are no known experiments on the effects of MDMA on flying—or even on driving. There ought to be some controlled studies, but alas, there aren't. It is possible that many general aviation mishaps have been brought on by MDMA abuse, and that will present a real problem for future [National Transportation Safety Board] NTSB investigations. But in the meantime it goes without saying that any military flyer who abuses MDMA or any other amphetamine is guaranteed immediate, permanent grounding. (What the legal system does with the abuser is another chapter.) None but the insane passenger would look forward to flying with an overconfident, impulsive, hallucinating pilot. Or a paranoid, depressed, clumsy one.

4

> "*Some papers minimise the impact of data that suggest Ecstasy exposure is not having any long-term effects.*"

Researchers Exaggerate the Dangers Associated with Ecstasy Use

Jon Cole, Harry Sumnall, and Charles Grob

In the following viewpoint Jon Cole, Harry Sumnall, and Charles Grob argue that many studies of Ecstasy's effects are inaccurate due to higher-than-typical dosages given to test animals. They also claim that experimenters are biased in choosing user and control groups for the studies. Moreover, the authors contend that researchers are pressured to publish only studies that show negative results from using Ecstasy and to ignore data that do not substantiate long-term harmful effects. Cole is Reader in Addictive Behavior at the University of Liverpool, England. Sumnall is a postdoctoral researcher at the University of Liverpool. Grob is the director of the Division of Child and Adolescent Psychiatry at the Harbor–University of California Los Angeles Medical Center.

As you read, consider the following questions:
1. How do the number of deaths due to Ecstasy use compare to the number of deaths from alcohol and tobacco use, as cited by the authors?
2. What is the most profound adverse reaction to Ecstasy, according to Cole, Sumnall, and Grob?
3. What is the "snowball technique," according to the authors?

Jon Cole, Harry Sumnall, and Charles Grob, "Sorted: Ecstasy," *The Psychologist*, vol. 15, September 2002, pp. 464–67. Copyright © 2002 by *The Psychologist*. Reproduced by permission.

Ecstasy use and raves are a cultural phenomenon. Their impact upon the 'Chemical Generation' is believed by some to be the defining moment of the late 1980s and early 1990s. Picking up on this the media, always fascinated by illegal drug use, have sensationalised the negative effects of Ecstasy. The media can perhaps be forgiven for this: sensationalism sells. But what about psychologists, as scientists? Are we also guilty of jumping to conclusions when the research is in fact plagued by experimental confounds?

Everyone's Taking . . . What?

All-night dancing with the aid of stimulant drugs is not new. It has been known since the emergence of cocaine in 1920s London, and has continued throughout most of the 20th century. The major difference today is the sheer numbers that are using Ecstasy and other 'dance drugs'. Surveys of young people's drug use has indicated that in the UK [United Kingdom] about 10 per cent of young adults aged between 15 and 29 have tried Ecstasy, although this figure jumps to around 90 per cent when the respondents are attending raves or nightclubs regularly.

Ecstasy is the colloquial name for the entactogen MDMA. It became a drug of abuse in the early 1980s in several areas of the US. In the mid- to late-1980s MDMA crossed the Atlantic and became part of the illegal drug scene.

As with all illegal drugs, purity became an important issue—now it is difficult to know for certain exactly what Ecstasy is. Ecstasy tablets are sold under brand names, such as White Dove or Mitsubishi, which refer to imprints stamped on the tablet. Manufacturers of Ecstasy constantly change their brand names because fraudulent copies rapidly follow the emergence of a new design. This has led to a plethora of designs and a corresponding problem in estimating the purity of Ecstasy tablets without a full chemical analysis.

Others drugs have masqueraded as MDMA (the most common being other entactogens), and other drugs have been mixed to produce an MDMA-like effect, such as ketamine and ephedrine. Some tablets contain either no active ingredients at all or legal drugs, such as pain killers. It is difficult in this context for anyone to know with any certainty the actual drug intake of an Ecstasy user.

Ecstasy has a high public profile due to the media coverage of deaths that have been associated with its use. The Office of National Statistics reports that in the UK between 1993 and 1997 there were 72 deaths due to Ecstasy. During the same period there were 158 deaths from amphetamines. In contrast, every year around 50,000 people die as result of their alcohol use and around 120,000 as a result of smoking. While every death from the use of drugs is an avoidable tragedy, the perceived 'safety' of Ecstasy has encouraged its use among young people.

If the statistics from the UK and the US are compared, the toxicological effects of MDMA become convoluted. The fatalities recorded for MDMA intoxication differ radically in both symptomatology and number between the US and the UK. In the former, if MDMA is found in the bloodstream after death then it is recorded as a cause of death, even if the primary cause was something entirely different, such as carbon monoxide poisoning or a fall. Even with this very broad inclusion criterion, the number of recorded fatalities due to MDMA is very low. In the UK, however, the picture is entirely different, as the majority of cases can be directly attributed to the use of MDMA or related drugs.

The most profound adverse reaction to MDMA is hyperthermia—with body temperatures reaching as high as 44°C—usually followed by multiple organ failure. The overwhelming majority of these adverse reactions have occurred at the weekend after using Ecstasy in raves or nightclubs, leading to the use of the term 'Saturday Night Fever' by staff at accident and emergency departments.

Harm-reduction literature in the 1990s advocated methods of reducing body temperature and replacing fluids lost through sweating. While this advice has undoubtedly reduced the incidence of overheating after taking Ecstasy, it has created a new problem. Misinterpretation of this advice by intoxicated users has led to a number of adverse reactions to unrestricted water intake. Too much water can lead to swelling of the brain and in some cases death.

Recently attention has moved away from the acute toxicity of Ecstasy. MDMA has been found to produce long-term changes in the structure and function of the brains of various species. These changes involve the neurotransmitter serotonin, and are typically characterised as degeneration of the fibres emerging from serotonergic cell bodies. The cell bodies themselves are unaffected. This has led to the classification of MDMA as a neurotoxin.

As the serotonergic cell bodies are spared and actually regenerate these fibres, some have questioned whether this classification is appropriate. These researchers advocate that a true neurotoxic effect involves the robust and well-validated biological measures of cell-body degeneration, changes that are not present after MDMA administration.

The "Evidence" Cannot Be Trusted

Nobody claims ecstasy is benign. It isn't, and never could be—no drug is. Yet few of the experts we contacted believe that research has yet proved ecstasy causes lasting damage to human brain cells or memory. Far from it, according to some, the highest-profile evidence to date simply cannot be trusted.

Blotchy brain scans of ecstasy users have become the ace card in public information campaigns. In the US, they also strongly influenced the move to tougher sentences. Yet impartial experts told us that the scans, though published in a respected journal, are based on experiments so fundamentally flawed they risk undermining the credibility of attempts to educate people about the risks of drugs. "The brain scans do not prove ecstasy damages serotonergic neurons," said one researcher, who asked for anonymity. "Whether to use the evidence is therefore a matter of politics rather than science."

David Concar, *New Scientist*, April 20, 2002.

Some also argue that the doses required to produce the long-term changes in the serotonergic system far exceed those used by recreational users. Most experiments looking at long-term changes in rats use a minimum of 40 mg/kg of MDMA administered as 10 mg/kg injections over six hours at two-hour intervals. Primate studies typically use a total of 40 mg/kg administered as 5 mg/kg injections over four consecutive days at 12-hour intervals. In both cases the dosing pattern is not typical of recreational Ecstasy users (who normally take about 1.9 mg/kg orally).

There is also strong evidence that injection of MDMA is two to three times more neurotoxic than oral administration in the primate. For example, squirrel monkeys given 2.5 mg/kg of MDMA orally every two weeks for four months did not show reduced serotonergic function.

But What About Humans?

The potential for neurotoxic effects of MDMA has led some researchers to investigate the long-term effects of Ecstasy in recreational dug users. The findings from these studies have been avidly reported by the media, particularly in magazines and programmes aimed at young people. There are many websites by Ecstasy users that report the results of such studies, suggesting that the users themselves are interested in their outcomes.

The general consensus in the media appears to be that Ecstasy causes long-term damage to recreational users. However, on closer inspection, there are methodological problems with these studies that preclude such a cause-and-effect relationship to be demonstrated unequivocally.

Sampling

Most studies looking at the long-term effects of Ecstasy use similar recruitment methods, with the most widely used being the 'snowball technique'. This involves getting participants to advertise the study to their peers: in particular their Ecstasy-using peers. In practice, this normally equates with a largely student-based population, as recruitment tends to occur in and around universities as part of final-year projects or doctoral theses. One can question whether these samples represent the population as a whole, as they are both self-selected and exclusive, largely consisting of people who have attained a certain academic level.

Given the high media profile of the long-term effects of Ecstasy, one must also question whether the participants are coming forward to confirm their fears about any adverse reactions that they may have suffered. In some studies there are even differences in the backgrounds between the Ecstasy users and their control group, for instance the control group displays a higher level of education. A more extreme example is the use of Ecstasy users from the UK in studies conducted in the US. As it is not reported in the relevant study where the participants actually came from, there is the possibility of cross-cultural contamination of the results. These inherent differences may have influenced the results obtained; for instance, participants with higher educational attainment are bound to obtain better scores on cognitive tests.

Lifestyle Factors

The typical design of a study investigating the long-term effects of Ecstasy is to compare a group of users to a group of non-users at a single time point and usually within three weeks of using Ecstasy. But Ecstasy users form a distinct subculture of individuals who attend raves and use dance drugs to aid their experience. Within this subculture it is very difficult to identify individuals who have *not* used Ecstasy, and there are therefore lifestyle factors that may explain the results.

One of the most common side-effects reported by this group of users is sleep disturbance, typically characterised by insomnia and accompanied by fatigue and exhaustion. This is possibly a result of staying awake all night and dancing while under the influence of Ecstasy and other drugs, although similar results have been obtained from clinical studies that involved administering MDMA during the day. Airline stewardesses exposed to repeated circadian disruption in a similar fashion to Ecstasy users report similar symptoms and have altered cognitive abilities. As the majority of the dance drugs are anorectic, another common side-effect is a reduced appetite and weight loss.

Both of these major side-effects would not be experienced by non-drug-using controls and represent non-drug-related differences between the groups. Also, controls who have used drugs other than Ecstasy may appear to control for non-Ecstasy drug use—but in fact they would be in a similar position to the non-drug-using controls (in that they have often not attended raves and been up all night dancing).

Psychopathology

Two broad types of psychopathology are associated with Ecstasy use in both case reports and surveys: panic attacks, anxiety, and psychotic reactions associated with acute intoxication; and depression associated with long-term use. But the majority of the community-based studies have failed to find a definitive cause-and-effect relationship between Ecstasy use and psychopathology, as these disorders are also found in non-Ecstasy users.

It is also known that most adult psychopathology begins to emerge during adolescence—when Ecstasy use in the UK also usually starts. Therefore it is impossible to accurately determine from retrospective self-reports whether the drug use preceded the onset of symptomatology. When users regularly read media reports of Ecstasy causing psychopathology, it is highly possible that their causal attributions may distort the temporal relationship between drug use and symptoms. . . .

So Are the Long-Term Effects of Ecstasy 'Iatrogenic'?

The pressure to publish positive results has meant that some papers minimise the impact of data that suggest Ecstasy exposure is not having any long-term effects. In these papers there are numerous tests run on the participants, but only the ones that work are reported in detail, while negative data are ignored . . . or only reported as meeting abstracts. This suggests that hypotheses concerning the long-term effects of Ecstasy are not being uniformly substantiated and lends support to the idea that Ecstasy is not causing long-term effects associated with a loss of serotonin.

The public health implications of potential MDMA-induced neurotoxicity are undoubtedly important. It is essential that the long-term effects of MDMA on recreational drug users are discovered. On the other hand, telling the 'Chemical Generation' that they are brain-damaged when they are not creates a public health problem. Effective harm reduction relies on accurate information being delivered to the user by a credible source. Misinterpretation of harm reduction information about Ecstasy has already had fatal consequences, and it is important that this is not repeated.

"One of the most detrimental long-term effects of heroin is addiction itself."

Heroin Is Addictive

National Institute on Drug Abuse

The National Institute on Drug Abuse (NIDA) supports research on drug abuse and addiction. The following viewpoint is an excerpt from its Research Report series on heroin abuse and addiction in which the authors maintain that heroin is a highly addictive drug that is abused by a diverse—and increasingly younger—group of users. Once heroin users become addicted, according to the institute, they spend more and more of their time and energy trying to satisfy their addiction. Addicts also experience many adverse short- and long-term effects from heroin use, such as impaired mental ability, risk of infections from sharing needles, and medical complications. However, drug abuse treatment programs can help heroin users kick their addiction, NIDA claims.

As you read, consider the following questions:

1. How many Americans have used heroin at some point in their lives, according to the 1998 National Household Survey on Drug Abuse cited by the authors?
2. Which method of administering heroin provides the greatest intensity and most rapid onset of euphoria, according to the report?
3. Why is heroin so addictive, according to the authors?

National Institute on Drug Abuse, "Heroin Abuse and Addiction," *National Institute on Drug Abuse Research Report*, September 2000.

Heroin is an illegal, highly addictive drug. It is both the most abused and the most rapidly acting of the opiates. Heroin is processed from morphine, a naturally occurring substance extracted from the seed pod of certain varieties of poppy plants. It is typically sold as a white or brownish powder or as the black sticky substance known on the streets as "black tar heroin." Although purer heroin is becoming more common, most street heroin is "cut" with other drugs or with substances such as sugar, starch, powdered milk, or quinine. Street heroin can also be cut with strychnine or other poisons. Because heroin abusers do not know the actual strength of the drug or its true contents, they are at risk of overdose or death. Heroin also poses special problems because of the transmission of HIV and other diseases that can occur from sharing needles or other injection equipment.

The Scope of Heroin Use in the United States

According to the 1998 National Household Survey on Drug Abuse, which may actually underestimate illicit opiate (heroin) use, an estimated 2.4 million people had used heroin at some time in their lives, and nearly 130,000 of them reported using it within the month preceding the survey. The survey report estimates that there were 81,000 new heroin users in 1997. A large proportion of these recent new users were smoking, snorting, or sniffing heroin, and most (87 percent) were under age 26. In 1992, only 61 percent were younger than 26.

The 1998 Drug Abuse Warning Network (DAWN), which collects data on drug-related hospital emergency department (ED) episodes from 21 metropolitan areas, estimates that 14 percent of all drug-related ED episodes involved heroin. Even more alarming is the fact that between 1991 and 1996, heroin-related ED episodes more than doubled (from 35,898 to 73,846). Among youths aged 12 to 17, heroin-related episodes nearly quadrupled.

NIDA's Community Epidemiology Work Group (CEWG), which provides information about the nature and patterns of drug use in 21 cities, reported in its December 1999 publication that heroin was mentioned most often as the primary drug of abuse in drug abuse treatment admissions in Baltimore, Boston, Los Angeles, Newark, New York, and San Francisco.

How Is Heroin Used?

Heroin is usually injected, sniffed/snorted, or smoked. Typically, a heroin abuser may inject up to four times a day. Intravenous injection provides the greatest intensity and most rapid onset of euphoria (7 to 8 seconds), while intramuscular injection produces a relatively slow onset of euphoria (5 to 8 minutes). When heroin is sniffed or smoked, peak effects are usually felt within 10 to 15 minutes. Although smoking and sniffing heroin do not produce a "rush" as quickly or as intensely as intravenous injection, NIDA researchers have confirmed that all three forms of heroin administration are addictive.

Injection continues to be the predominant method of heroin use among addicted users seeking treatment; however, researchers have observed a shift in heroin use patterns, from injection to sniffing and smoking. In fact, sniffing/snorting heroin is now the most widely reported means of taking heroin among users admitted for drug treatment in Newark, Chicago, and New York.

With the shift in heroin abuse patterns comes an even more

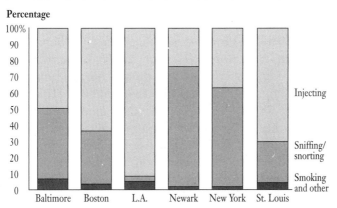

Route of Administration Among Heroin Treatment Admissions in Selected Areas

Percentage

Community Epidemiology Work Group, NIDA, December 1999.

diverse group of users. Older users (over 30) continue to be one of the largest user groups in most national data. However, the increase continues in new, young users across the country who are being lured by inexpensive, high-purity heroin that can be sniffed or smoked instead of injected. Heroin has also been appearing in more affluent communities.

The Short-Term Effects of Heroin Use

Soon after injection (or inhalation), heroin crosses the blood-brain barrier. In the brain, heroin is converted to morphine and binds rapidly to opioid receptors. Abusers typically report feeling a surge of pleasurable sensation, a "rush." The intensity of the rush is a function of how much drug is taken and how rapidly the drug enters the brain and binds to the natural opioid receptors. Heroin is particularly addictive because it enters the brain so rapidly. With heroin, the rush is usually accompanied by a warm flushing of the skin, dry mouth, and a heavy feeling in the extremities, which may be accompanied by nausea, vomiting, and severe itching.

After the initial effects, abusers usually will be drowsy for several hours. Mental function is clouded by heroin's effect on the central nervous system. Cardiac function slows. Breathing is also severely slowed, sometimes to the point of death. Heroin overdose is a particular risk on the street, where the amount and purity of the drug cannot be accurately known.

The Long-Term Effects

One of the most detrimental long-term effects of heroin is addiction itself. Addiction is a chronic, relapsing disease, characterized by compulsive drug seeking and use, and by neurochemical and molecular changes in the brain. Heroin also produces profound degrees of tolerance and physical dependence, which are also powerful motivating factors for compulsive use and abuse. As with abusers of any addictive drug, heroin abusers gradually spend more and more time and energy obtaining and using the drug. Once they are addicted, the heroin abusers' primary purpose in life becomes seeking and using drugs. The drugs literally change their brains.

Physical dependence develops with higher doses of the

drug. With physical dependence, the body adapts to the presence of the drug and withdrawal symptoms occur if use is reduced abruptly. Withdrawal may occur within a few hours after the last time the drug is taken. Symptoms of withdrawal include restlessness, muscle and bone pain, insomnia, diarrhea, vomiting, cold flashes with goose bumps ("cold turkey"), and leg movements. Major withdrawal symptoms peak between 24 and 48 hours after the last dose of heroin and subside after about a week. However, some people have shown persistent withdrawal signs for many months. Heroin withdrawal is never fatal to otherwise healthy adults, but it can cause death to the fetus of a pregnant addict.

At some point during continuous heroin use, a person can become addicted to the drug. Sometimes addicted individuals will endure many of the withdrawal symptoms to reduce their tolerance for the drug so that they can again experience the rush.

Physical dependence and the emergence of withdrawal symptoms were once believed to be the key features of heroin addiction. We now know this may not be the case entirely, since craving and relapse can occur weeks and months after withdrawal symptoms are long gone. We also know that patients with chronic pain who need opiates to function (sometimes over extended periods) have few if any problems leaving opiates after their pain is resolved by other means. This may be because the patient in pain is simply seeking relief of pain and not the rush sought by the addict.

Medical Complications

Medical consequences of chronic heroin abuse include scarred and/or collapsed veins, bacterial infections of the blood vessels and heart valves, abscesses (boils) and other soft-tissue infections, and liver or kidney disease. Lung complications (including various types of pneumonia and tuberculosis) may result from the poor health condition of the abuser as well as from heroin's depressing effects on respiration. Many of the additives in street heroin may include substances that do not readily dissolve and result in clogging the blood vessels that lead to the lungs, liver, kidneys, or brain. This can cause infection or even death of small patches of cells in vital organs.

Immune reactions to these or other contaminants can cause arthritis or other rheumatologic problems.

Of course, sharing of injection equipment or fluids can lead to some of the most severe consequences of heroin abuse—infections with hepatitis B and C, HIV, and a host of other blood-borne viruses, which drug abusers can then pass on to their sexual partners and children.

Short- and Long-Term Effects of Heroin Abuse

Short-Term Effects:	Long-Term Effects:
"Rush"	Addiction
Depressed respiration	Infectious diseases, for example, HIV/AIDS and hepatitis B and C
Clouded mental functioning	Collapsed veins
	Bacteria infections
Nausea and vomiting	Abscesses
Suppression of pain	Infection of heart lining and valves
Spontaneous abortion	Arthritis and other rheumatologic problems

Heroin Abuse and Pregnant Women

Heroin abuse can cause serious complications during pregnancy, including miscarriage and premature delivery. Children born to addicted mothers are at greater risk of SIDS (sudden infant death syndrome), as well. Pregnant women should not be detoxified from opiates because of the increased risk of spontaneous abortion or premature delivery; rather, treatment with methadone is strongly advised. Although infants born to mothers taking prescribed methadone may show signs of physical dependence, they can be treated easily and safely in the nursery. Research has demonstrated also that the effects of in utero exposure to methadone are relatively benign.

Other Risks

Heroin addicts are at risk for contracting HIV, hepatitis C, and other infectious diseases. Drug abusers may become infected with HIV, hepatitis C, and other blood-borne pathogens through sharing and reuse of syringes and injection paraphernalia that have been used by infected individuals. They may also become infected with HIV and, although less often, to hepatitis C through unprotected sexual contact with an infected person. Injection drug use has been a factor in an estimated one-third of all HIV and more than half of all hepatitis C cases in the nation. NIDA-funded research has found that drug abusers can change the behaviors that put them at risk for contracting HIV, through drug abuse treatment, prevention, and community-based outreach programs. They can eliminate drug use, drug-related risk behaviors such as needle sharing, unsafe sexual practices, and, in turn, the risk of exposure to HIV/AIDS and other infectious diseases. Drug abuse prevention and treatment are highly effective in preventing the spread of HIV.

"Heroin is neither irresistible nor inescapable. Only a very small share of the population ever uses it, and a large majority of those who do never become addicted."

Heroin Users Do Not Always Become Addicted

Jacob Sullum

Jacob Sullum is a syndicated columnist and the author of *Saying Yes: In Defense of Drug Use*, from which the following viewpoint is excerpted. Sullum argues that society's acceptance of alcohol and tobacco—but not of drugs such as heroin—is hypocritical. Alcohol and tobacco are responsible for many more deaths than heroin is, he claims. Furthermore, according to Sullum, just as the majority of people who drink alcohol are not alcoholics, the majority of heroin users are not drug addicts. He argues that numerous studies have found that most heroin users are able to work at productive jobs while using the drug on weekends or at parties.

As you read, consider the following questions:

1. What are the common withdrawal symptoms experienced by heroin addicts who abruptly stop using the drug, according to Sullum?
2. What percentage of the U.S. population used heroin in 2001, as cited by the author?
3. What is an important deterrent to excessive heroin use, according to a British study cited by Sullum?

The conventional wisdom about heroin, which shapes the popular understanding of addiction, is nicely summed up in the journalist Martin Booth's 1996 history of opium. "Addiction is the compulsive taking of drugs which have such a hold over the addict he or she cannot stop using them without suffering severe symptoms and even death," he writes. "Opiate dependence . . . is as fundamental to an addict's existence as food and water, a physio-chemical fact: an addict's body is chemically reliant upon its drug for opiates actually alter the body's chemistry so it cannot function properly without being periodically primed. A hunger for the drug forms when the quantity in the bloodstream falls below a certain level. . . . Fail to feed the body and it deteriorates and may die from drug starvation." Booth also declares that "everyone . . . is a potential addict"; that "addiction can start with the very first dose"; and that "with continued use addiction is a certainty."

Booth's description, which passed muster with his editors in England and the United States, probably fit the preconceptions of most readers. Yet it is wrong or grossly misleading in every particular. To understand why is to recognize the fallacies underlying a reductionist, drug-centered view of addiction in which chemicals force themselves on people—a view that iconoclasts such as Stanton Peele and maverick psychiatrist Thomas Szasz have long criticized. The idea that a drug can compel the person who consumes it to continue consuming it, in essence forcing him to be a glutton, is the most important tenet of voodoo pharmacology, because this power makes possible all the other evils to which drug use supposedly leads.

Withdrawal Penalty

In Booth's gloss, as in other popular portrayals, the potentially fatal agony of withdrawal is the gun that heroin holds to the addict's head. These accounts greatly exaggerate both the severity and the importance of withdrawal symptoms. Heroin addicts who abruptly stop using the drug commonly report flu-like symptoms, which may include chills, sweating, runny nose and eyes, muscular aches, stomach cramps, nausea, diarrhea, or headaches. While certainly unpleasant, the experience is not life-threatening. Indeed, addicts who have developed tolerance (needing higher doses to achieve the same effect) often voluntarily undergo withdrawal so they can begin using heroin again at a lower level, thereby reducing the cost of their habit. Another sign that fear of withdrawal symptoms is not the essence of addiction is the fact that heroin users commonly drift in and out of their habits, going through periods of abstinence and returning to the drug long after any physical discomfort has faded away. Indeed, the observation that detoxification is not tantamount to overcoming an addiction, that addicts typically will try repeatedly before successfully kicking the habit, is a commonplace of drug treatment. . . .

Simply Irresistible?

Even if addiction is not a physical compulsion, perhaps some drug experiences are so alluring that people find it impossible to resist them. Certainly that is heroin's reputation, encapsulated in the title of a 1972 book: *It's So Good, Don't Even Try It Once.* When Martin Booth tells us that anyone can be addicted to heroin, that it may take just one dose, and that it will certainly happen to you if you're foolish enough to repeat the experiment, he is drawing on a long tradition of anti-drug propaganda. . . . The original model for such warnings was not heroin but alcohol. The dry crusaders of the nineteenth and early twentieth centuries taught that every tippler was a potential drunkard, that a glass of beer was the first step on the road to ruin, and that repeated use of distilled spirits made addiction virtually inevitable. Today, when a wrecked kitchen is supposed to symbolize the havoc caused by a snort of heroin, similar assumptions about opiates are even more widely held, and they likewise are based more on faith than facts.

The fact that heroin use is so rare—involving, according to the government's data, something like 0.2 percent of the U.S. population in 2001—suggests that its appeal is much more limited than we've been led to believe. If heroin really is "so good," why does it have such a tiny share of the illegal drug market? Marijuana is more than forty-five times as popular. The National Household Survey on Drug Abuse indicates that about 3 million Americans have used heroin, 15 percent of them in the last year and 4 percent in the last month. These numbers suggest that the vast majority of heroin users either never become addicted or, if they do, manage to give the drug up. A survey of high school seniors found that 1 percent had used heroin in the previous year, while 0.1 percent had used it on twenty or more days in the previous month. Assuming that daily use is a reasonable proxy for opiate addiction, one in ten of the students who had taken heroin in the last year might have qualified as addicts. These are not the sort of numbers you'd expect for a drug that's irresistible. . . .

Tobacco

The same study found that 32 percent of tobacco users had experienced substance dependence. Figures like that one are the basis for the claim that nicotine is "more addictive than heroin." After all, cigarette smokers typically go through a pack or so a day, so they're under the influence of nicotine every waking moment. Heroin users typically do not use their drug even once a day. Smokers offended by this comparison are quick to point out that they function fine, meeting their responsibilities at work and home, despite their habit. This, they assume, is impossible for heroin users. We'll take a closer look at that assumption later, but it's true that nicotine's psychoactive effects are easier to reconcile with the requirements of everyday life. Indeed, nicotine can actually enhance concentration and improve performance on certain tasks. So one important reason why most cigarette smokers consume their drug throughout the day is that they can do so without running into trouble. And because they're used to smoking in so many different settings, they may find nicotine harder to give up than a drug they use only with certain people in secret. . . .

Although many smokers have a hard time quitting, those who succeed generally do so without formal treatment. Surprisingly, the same may also be true of heroin addicts. In the early 1960s, based on records kept by the Federal Bureau of Narcotics, the sociologist Charles Winick concluded that narcotic addicts tend to "mature out" of the habit in their thirties. He suggested that "addiction may be a self-limiting process for perhaps two-thirds of addicts." Subsequent researchers have questioned Winick's assumptions, and other studies have come up with lower estimates. But it's clear that "natural recovery" is much more common than the public has been led to believe. In a 1974 study of Vietnam veterans, only 12 percent of those who were addicted to heroin in Vietnam took up the habit again during the three years after their return to the United States. (This was not because they couldn't find heroin; half of them used it at least once after their return, generally without becoming addicted again.) Those who had undergone treatment (half of the group) were just as likely to be re-addicted as those who had not. Since those with stronger addictions were more likely to receive treatment, this does not necessarily mean that treatment was useless, but it clearly was not a prerequisite for giving up heroin.

Heroin Is Safe

Heroin is safe when prescribed and consumed under sanitary, controlled conditions. Unlike cigarettes and alcohol, it does not destroy human organs. The "high" of heroin, for many experienced consumers, is neither intoxicating like alcohol nor tranquilizing like benzodiazepams. Perhaps the closest analogy is to "smoke-free" cigarettes that deliver a dose of nicotine with fewer associated tars and other carcinogens. Thousands of people have held and/or hold responsible jobs while injecting heroin two or three times per day.

Ethan Nadelmann, *Cannabis Science: From Prohibition to Human Right*, 1997.

Despite its reputation, then, heroin is neither irresistible nor inescapable. Only a very small share of the population ever uses it, and a large majority of those who do never become addicted. Even within the minority who develop a daily habit, most manage to stop using heroin, often without professional intervention. Yet heroin remains the paradigmatic voodoo drug, ineluctably turning its users into zombies who must obey its commands. . . .

The idea that drugs cause addiction was rejected in the case of alcohol because it was so clearly at odds with everyday experience, which showed that the typical drinker was not an alcoholic. But what Bruce Alexander calls "the myth of drug-induced addiction" is still widely accepted in the case of heroin—and, by extension, the drugs compared to it—because moderate opiate users are hard to find. That does not mean they don't exist; indeed, judging from the government's survey results, they are a lot more common than addicts. It's just that people who use opiates in a controlled way are inconspicuous by definition, and keen to remain so.

In the early 1960s, however, researchers began to tentatively identify users of heroin and other opiates who were not addicts. "Surprisingly enough," one psychiatrist wrote in 1961, "in some cases at least, narcotic use may be confined to weekends or parties and the users may be able to continue in gainful employment for some time. Although this pattern often deteriorates and the rate of use increases, several cases have been observed in which relatively gainful and steady employment has been maintained for two to three years while the user was on what might be called a regulated or controlled habit."

A few years later, Norman Zinberg and David C. Lewis described five categories of narcotic users, including "people who use narcotics regularly but who develop little or no tolerance for them and do not suffer withdrawal symptoms." They explained that "such people are usually able to work regularly and productively. They value the relaxation and the 'kick' obtained from the drug, but their fear of needing more and more of the drug to get the same kick causes them to impose rigorous controls on themselves."

Controlled Users

The example offered by Zinberg and Lewis was a forty-seven-year-old physician with a successful practice who had been injecting morphine four times a day, except weekends, for twelve years. He experienced modest discomfort on Saturdays and Sundays, when he abstained, but he stuck to his schedule and did not raise his dose except on occasions when he was especially busy or tense. Zinberg and Lewis's account suggests that morphine's main function for him was stress relief: "Somewhat facetiously, when describing his intolerance of people making emotional demands on him, he said that he took one shot for his patients, one for his mistress, one for his family and one to sleep. He expressed no guilt about his drug taking, and made it clear that he had no intention of stopping."

Zinberg eventually interviewed sixty-one controlled opiate users. His criteria excluded both dabblers (the largest group of people who have used heroin) and daily users. One subject, for example, was a forty-one-year-old carpenter who had used heroin on weekends for a decade. Married sixteen years, he lived with his wife and three children in a middle-class suburb. Another was a twenty-seven-year-old college student studying special education. He had used heroin two or three times a month for three years, then once a week for a year. The controlled users said they liked "the 'rush' (glow or warmth), the sense of distance from their problems, and the tranquilizing powers of the drug." Opiate use was generally seen as a social activity, and it was often combined with other forms of recreation. Summing up the lessons he learned from his research, Zinberg emphasized the importance of self-imposed rules dictating when, where, and with whom the drug would be used.

Other researchers have reported similar findings. After interviewing twelve occasional heroin users, one concluded that "it seems possible for young people from a number of different backgrounds, family patterns, and educational abilities to use heroin occasionally without becoming addicted." The subjects typically took heroin with one or more friends, and the most frequently reported benefit was relaxation. One subject, a twenty-three-year-old graduate student, said it was "like taking a vacation from yourself. . . . When things get to you, it's a way of getting away without getting away." These occasional users were unanimous in rejecting addiction as inconsistent with their self-images. A British study of fifty-one opiate users likewise found that distaste for the junkie lifestyle was an important deterrent to excessive use. . . .

Legal Complications

Although not every addict resembles the shifty, shiftless thieves portrayed on TV, the Vietnam veterans study did find that crime and other "social adjustment problems" were more common among regular heroin users. This does not necessarily mean that heroin use caused these problems. Using a questionnaire designed to assess early warning signs of antisocial behavior, the researchers determined that "the men who used heroin were those who were especially disposed to adjustment problems even before they used the drug." While regular heroin use seemed to have an additional effect, it wasn't clear whether this was "because of the drug itself or because of its legal status."

Both of these complications make it hard to assess heroin's direct contribution to the problems heavy users often experience or cause: Troubled or antisocial people may be especially attracted to the drug, and its legal status makes it more dangerous to use. The law's role goes beyond the risk of arrest and the handicap of a criminal record. The drug's legal status helps make it the focus of an oppositional identity—the junkie at odds with straight society—that users who have little else to define themselves with are reluctant to give up. As the sociologist Harold Alksne and his colleagues suggested in the late 1960s, "the process of becoming an addict and being an addict in our culture may well be as much a social process and condition as it is physical and psychological." The importance of heroin addiction as a basis for identity is perhaps best illustrated by "pseudo-junkies," who claim to be addicted even though they have only dabbled in the drug. Then, too, the difficulty of obtaining heroin creates anxiety that would not exist if it were readily available, so that many addicts organize their lives around getting the next fix. Users are exposed to violence because they have to get the drug from criminals. The artificially high price of heroin, perhaps forty or fifty times what it would otherwise cost, may lead to heavy debts, housing problems, poor nutrition, and theft. The inflated cost also encourages users to inject the drug, a more efficient but riskier mode of administration. The legal treatment of injection equipment, including restrictions on distribution and penalties for possession, encourages needle sharing, which spreads diseases such as AIDS and hepatitis. The unreliable quality and unpredictable purity associated with the black market can lead to poisoning and accidental overdoses.

Minimal Risks

Without prohibition, then, a daily heroin habit would be far less burdensome and hazardous. Heroin itself is much less likely to kill a user than the reckless combination of heroin with other depressants, such as alcohol or barbiturates. The federal government's Drug Abuse Warning Network counted 4,820 mentions of heroin or morphine (which are indistinguishable in the blood) by medical examiners in 1999. Only 438 of these deaths (9 percent) were listed as directly caused by an overdose of the opiate. Three-quarters of the deaths were caused by heroin/morphine in combination with other drugs. Provided the user avoids such mixtures, has access to a supply of reliable purity, and follows sanitary injection procedures, the health risks of long-term opiate consumption are minimal.

The psychological and spiritual consequences are harder to assess. An occasional "vacation from yourself" is one thing, a perpetual holiday something else. A drug that makes you feel everything's OK has obvious perils, especially when it's not. Such a drug can help you avoid problems that ought to be dealt with and ease the discontent that might otherwise impel you to improve your situation. Even addicts who stay healthy and make an honest living may later regret the time and opportunities they wasted.

Then again, it's widely accepted, even by the same people who see heroin addiction as an unmitigated evil, that some individuals suffer from biochemical imbalances that make them unhappy. These imbalances, we're told, can and should be treated with drugs. As Thomas Szasz and other critics of psychiatry have observed, such beliefs create a double standard: If an unhappy person takes heroin, he is committing a crime. If he takes Prozac, he is treating his depression.

"*[Steroids] can induce irritability and aggression. . . . [They] may also induce a sense of invincibility and promote excessively macho behavior—and occasionally, attacks of rage or psychosis.*"

Steroids Are Dangerous

Steven Ungerleider

Steroids are natural and man-made supplements that enhance an athlete's performance. In the following viewpoint Steven Ungerleider asserts that steroid use is becoming more pervasive in sports, especially among middle and high school athletes. He maintains that while steroid use may increase an athlete's endurance and enhance muscle growth, it also has many risky side effects, such as aggression and high blood pressure. He recommends that health-care professionals educate youth about the dangers of steroid use to prevent the potentially fatal consequences of steroid abuse. Ungerleider is a sports psychologist, psychology consultant to the U.S. Olympic Committee, and author of several books on sports training.

As you read, consider the following questions:
1. What are all anabolic-androgenic steroids derived from, according to Ungerleider?
2. What factors are leading young athletes to try steroids, in Ungerleider's opinion?
3. What happened when Adolf Hitler's SS troops took steroids, according to the author?

S everal years ago, in a well-known research project, elite athletes were asked whether they would take a pill that guaranteed an Olympic gold medal if they knew it would kill them within a year. More than half of the athletes said they would take the pill.

The need to win at all costs has permeated many areas of our lives. In sports, one of the forms it takes is the use of anabolic-androgenic steroids (AAS). "Anabolic" refers to constructive metabolism or muscle-building, and "androgenic" means masculinizing. All AAS are derived from the hormone testosterone, which is found primarily in men, although women also produce it in smaller concentrations. There are at least thirty AAS, some natural and some synthetic.

Pervasive Use

Use of these substances has been pervasive for years among collegiate, Olympic, and professional competitors. Experiments with steroids began in Germany in the thirties, and their use by East German Olympic athletes is well known. More than 10,000 East German athletes in 22 events were given these synthetic hormones over 30 years. In August 2000, after a long battle in the criminal courts, more than 400 doctors, coaches, and trainers from the former East Germany were convicted of giving steroids to minors without their informed consent. But despite these revelations and convictions, scandals persist. . . . The chief of sports medicine for the United States Olympic Committee resigned in June 2000 in protest, saying that "some of our greatest Olympians have been using performance-enhancing drugs for years, and we have not been honest about our drug testing protocols."

Now anabolic steroids are becoming available to middle school and high school children as well. Concerns about body image and athletic performance lead adolescents to use the substances despite their serious side effects. Young athletes are responding to encouragement, social pressure, and their own desire to excel, as well as admonitions from coaches to put on muscle and build strength and resilience.

A recent survey by the National Institute on Drug Abuse indicates that steroid use by eighth- and tenth-graders is increasing, and twelfth-graders are increasingly likely to underestimate their risks. Some 2.7% of eighth- and tenth-graders and 2.9% of twelfth-graders admitted they had taken steroids at least once—a significant increase since 1991, the first year that full data were available. Other studies suggest that as many as 6% of high school students have used steroids. The numbers are especially alarming because many students will not admit that they take drugs. Sixth-graders report that these drugs are available in schoolyards, and they are increasingly used by nonathletes as well to impress their peers and attract the opposite sex.

Three Classes of Steroids

Anabolic-androgenic steroids fall into three classes: C-17 alkyl derivatives of testosterone; esters or derivatives of 19-nortestosterone; and esters of testosterone.

C-17 alkyl derivatives are soluble in water and can be taken orally. Among them are Anavar, Anadrol, Dianabol (a favorite among Olympians), and the most famous, Winstrol, also known as stanozolol. Stanozolol was taken in large doses by the Canadian sprint champion Ben Johnson, who was stripped of a gold medal in the 1988 Olympics. These steroids are often favored by athletes trying to avoid drug screens because they clear the body quickly (within a month).

The 19-nortestosterone derivatives are oil-based; they are usually injected and absorbed into fat deposits, where long-term energy is stored. The most popular steroid in this group is nandrolone (Deca-Durabolin). It has recently made headlines because it is found in food supplements and other preparations that can be bought without a prescription. Many athletes who test positive for nandrolone say they had no idea what was in the vitamin supplements they took. Because nandrolone is stored in fatty tissue and released over a long period of time, it may take 8–10 months to clear the body.

Esters of testosterone, the third class, are especially dangerous. Among them are testosterone propionate, Testex, and cypionate. Active both orally and by injection, they closely mimic the effects of natural testosterone and are therefore difficult to detect on drug screens. The International Olympic Committee determines their presence by measuring the ratio

Side Effects of Anabolic-Androgenic Steroids

In men:
- Gynecomastia (breast development), usually permanent
- Testicular or scrotal pain
- Testicular atrophy and decreased sperm production
- Premature baldness, even in adolescents
- Enlargement of the prostate gland, causing difficult urination

In women:
- Enlargement of the clitoris, usually irreversible
- Disruption of the menstrual cycle
- Permanent deepening of the voice
- Excessive facial and body hair

In both sexes:
- Nervous tension
- Aggressiveness and antisocial behavior
- Paranoia and psychotic states
- Acne, often serious enough to leave permanent scars on the face and body
- Burning and pain during urination
- Gastrointestinal and leg muscle cramps
- Headaches
- Dizziness
- High blood pressure
- Heart, kidney, and liver damage
- In adolescents, premature end to the growth of long bones, leading to shortened stature

of testosterone to the related substance epitestosterone in an athlete's urine; if the ratio exceeds 6:1, the athlete is suspected of cheating.

Steroids' Effects

How do anabolic steroids work? The scientific literature demonstrates their effects, but it is not clear how they enhance the synthesis of proteins and the growth of muscles. They apparently increase endurance, allowing longer periods of exercise, and improve the results of strength training by increasing both the size (mass) of muscles and the number of muscle fibers.

Especially when taken in high doses, AAS can induce irritability and aggression. When Hitler's SS troops took steroids to build strength and stave off fatigue, they found that the hormones also made them more fearless and willing to fight. Among young athletic warriors today, steroids not only permit harder training and faster recovery from long workouts but may also induce a sense of invincibility and promote excessively macho behavior—and occasionally, attacks of rage or psychosis.

These drugs have a great many other risks as well. Men may develop reduced sperm production, shrunken testicles, impotence, and irreversible breast enlargement. Women may develop deep voices and excessive body hair. In either sex, baldness and acne are risks. The ratio of good to bad lipids may change, increasing the danger of heart attacks, strokes, and liver cancer. In adolescents bone growth may stop prematurely. Injecting steroids with contaminated needles creates a risk of HIV and other blood-borne infections.

Mental health professionals must consider how to address this problem in our schools. The National Institute on Drug Abuse and its nongovernmental partners have established Web sites to educate youth about the dangers of steroids. These sites may be found at steroidabuse.org, archpediatrics.com, and drugabuse.gov. A useful site for professionals interested in intervention and prevention is tpronline.org. Researchers at the Oregon Health Sciences University have devised an effective program known as Adolescents Training and Learning to Avoid Steroids (ATLAS). It is a team-centered and gender-specific approach that educates athletes about the dangers of steroids and other drugs while providing alternatives including nutritional advice and strength training. A three-year study demonstrated the benefits of the program for 3,000 football players in 31 Oregon high schools. ATLAS reduced not only anabolic steroid use but also alcohol and illicit drug use and drunk driving. Still more research is needed both to address the potentially deadly consequences of youthful steroid use and to discover ways of preventing it.

"Perfectly legal substances such as alcohol, cigarettes, and fatty foods are even more damaging to people's health than steroid precursors, but our society has not seen fit to ban adult use of them yet."

Steroids Are Not as Dangerous as Many Experts Claim

Ronald Bailey

Steroids have been used for more than one hundred years as a way to improve athletic performance. In the following viewpoint Ronald Bailey contends that the sale and use of steroids is not a social emergency that requires intervention by the federal government. The risks associated with steroid use are less harmful than generally believed, he asserts. He argues that the majority of steroid consumers use the substance responsibly, and those who commit crimes while under the influence of steroids can be held accountable for their actions by laws and institutions already in place. Bailey is the science reporter for *Reason* magazine.

As you read, consider the following questions:

1. When did the federal government outlaw the sale of steroids used for nonmedical purposes, according to Bailey?
2. What are some legal substances that are even more damaging to people's health than steroid precursors, in the author's opinion?
3. What is Bailey's response to those who claim that steroids harm children?

*T*he *New York Times* and *The Washington Post* are now flog-
ging the latest drug crisis—over-the-counter steroid precursors.

Steroids and Their Precursors

Steroids are a class of compounds that mimic the effects of the
male sex hormone testosterone. The pre-modern era (circa
1880) of steroids initiated by French physiologist Charles
Edouard Brown-Sequard involved injecting crushed dog and
guinea pig testicles. Scientists in the 1930s succeeded in syn-
thesizing testosterone. Supplementary steroid use began ex-
panding in the 1950s, when Soviet Olympic athletes started
using it to improve their performance. Since 1990, the Federal government has outlawed the sale of a variety of steroids
except for medical purposes.

Since 1990, clever chemists, working for the supplement
industry, have devised compounds which they claim are precursors to testosterone. And by now anyone connected to
the Internet has been spammed hundreds of times with
emails touting the effectiveness of these precursors in building muscle and reducing fat. Does the sale of over-the-
counter steroid supplements constitute a societal emergency
requiring intervention by the Feds? No. "Where is the societal damage?" asked supplement company Syntrax Innova-
tions' founder Derek Cornelius in *The Washington Post*.
"[Critics] would have a point if people were having bad side
effects, if people were dying in hospitals, but it's not happening. It's like making an issue out of something that's not."

However, steroids and their precursors do have some negative side effects that vary among users depending on how
much they use and their specific genetics. Short-term effects
include acne and shrunken testicles (which are generally re-
versed after users stop taking the supplements). Long-term
effects may include stunted growth in teenagers, liver damage, enhanced risk of heart disease and prostate cancer. But
these are not unusual risks. People balance these types of
risks versus benefits all the time.

Of course perfectly legal substances such as alcohol,
cigarettes, and fatty foods are even more damaging to people's
health than steroid precursors, but our society has not seen fit

to ban adult use of them yet (though a cadre of health puritans is working ceaselessly to do just that).

What about the children? Our society has had no problem imposing limits on access to alcohol to people under age 21 and cigarettes to those under age 18. Similar restrictions could be established if steroid precursors are shown to be truly harmful to teenagers. One should not infantilize society by using possible harm to children as an excuse to deny adults access to products and services they can appropriately and safely use.

Other Drugs Are More Dangerous than Steroids

Isn't it time for the brainwashed public to know the truth about steroids? In their ideological zeal to ban "performance enhancing" drugs, national governments and the various local and international sports federations have ignorantly and self-righteously declared that steroid use is cheating, dangerous, and stupid. In fact, in general, it is neither dangerous nor stupid and it is cheating only because it has been capriciously commanded to be so.

In the first place, with respect to the alleged danger, people ought to know that there are dozens of steroids and it would be absurd to imagine that their risks are identical. Moreover, steroids come in two broad classes—the orals and the injectables. It is true that most of the orals have associated hazards but not a single one of them is as hazardous as smoking or drinking. The principal dangers of the injectables result from overdosing and, even so, [they] are mainly such alarming matters as acne and severe headache. Every legally obtainable prescription drug comes with a warning of dozens of worse side effects.

Sidney Gendin, "Ban Athletes Who Don't Use Steroids," www. mesomorphosis.com, 2002.

But what if supplement manufacturers defraud consumers? We already have plenty of laws and agencies that are fully empowered to protect consumers against fraud.

The question comes down to whether people can be trusted to use such substances responsibly. The answer, of course, is that not everyone will. But that does not mean that the majority of those who would behave responsibly should be forbidden access to enhancements that they regard as beneficial.

Roid Rage

For example, there is evidence that overuse of steroidal substances causes some few people to become excessively aggressive, the so-called "roid rage" phenomenon. However, we hold drunks responsible for their actions; similarly society should have no difficulty holding roid ragers accountable. In fact, *The New York Times* underscores this point when it notes that steroid user Patrick Keogan stopped taking it after he became so angry during a traffic incident that he allowed his car to drift away while he argued with another motorist. Clearly users like Keogan can and do take responsibility for their actions.

Private sports organizations like the International Olympics Committee and the National Football League certainly have the right to ban their athletes from using steroid precursors if they wish, but they don't have the right to ask the Feds to take care of their policing problems by banning the use of steroids by ordinary citizens who want to lose fat or look better.

On the evidence marshaled so far by supplement critics, the bottom line is that we don't need to open a new anti-steroid front in an already highly destructive and failing War on Drugs.

Periodical Bibliography

The following articles have been selected to supplement the diverse views presented in this chapter.

Virginia Berridge	"Altered States: Opium and Tobacco Compared," *Social Research*, Fall 2001.
Alexander Cockburn	"The Right Not to Be in Pain,"*Nation*, February 3, 2003.
Laura D'Angelo	"Close-Up: Ecstasy," *Scholastic Choices*, February 2003.
Patti Davis	"Dope: A Love Story," *Time*, May 7, 2001.
John DiConsiglio	"Hooked on Heroin," *Junior Scholastic*, April 25, 2003.
Economist	"The Agony and the Ecstasy: Recreational Drugs," September 7, 2002.
Luke Fisher	"Marijuana as Medicine," *Maclean's*, October 14, 2002.
D.A. Frank et al.	"The Crack Baby Myth," *Harvard Mental Health Letter*, September 2001.
Lester Grinspoon	"The Harmfulness Tax," *Social Research*, Fall 2001.
Robert Maccoun and Peter Reuter	"Marijuana, Heroin, and Cocaine: The War on Drugs May Be a Disaster, but Do We Really Want a Legalized Peace?" *American Prospect*, June 3, 2002.
Dayn Perry	"Pumped-Up Hysteria," *Reason*, January 2003.
Sara Rimensnyder	"The Feds vs. Medical Pot: One Toke over the Line," *Reason*, March 2002.
Sue Rusche and Marsha Rosenbaum	"Do Efforts to Legalize Marijuana for Medical Use Encourage Teen Drug Use?" *CQ Researcher*, March 15, 2002.
Jacob Sullum	"High Road: Is Marijuana a 'Gateway'?" *Reason*, March 2003.
Jacob Sullum	"H: The Surprising Truth about Heroin and Addiction," *Reason*, June 2003.
Clare Wilson	"Fixed Up: When Nothing Else Works, Heroin Addicts Should Be Prescribed the Drug They Crave," *New Scientist*, March 30, 2002.

CHAPTER 2

What Causes Drug Abuse and Addiction?

Chapter Preface

Researchers have discovered that most people who struggle with drug addiction began experimenting with drugs in their teens. In consequence, discovering how many teens take drugs, determining the age when drug use typically begins, and finding out why young people become interested in drugs is critical to addressing the problem of addiction. The 2002 Partnership Attitude Tracking Study (PATS) estimates that there are 23.6 million teenagers in grades seven through twelve in the United States. According to the 2002 study, slightly less than half the teens (48 percent) admitted to trying illegal drugs at least once in their life, more than a third (37 percent) used illegal drugs in the last year, and nearly a quarter (24 percent) used illegal drugs in the past month. However, the study found that illegal drug use among teenagers had fallen since 1997, when 53 percent of teens had tried an illegal drug.

According to the 2003 PATS survey (which asked slightly different questions than the 2002 study), the most popular illicit drug for high school seniors is alcohol (78 percent of seniors have tried it), followed by cigarettes (57 percent). Marijuana is the most popular illegal drug (33 percent), followed by inhalants (17 percent). The percentage of teens who have tried crack/cocaine, methamphetamines, and Ecstasy are roughly equal, at 9 percent. LSD use is at 6 percent, while heroin and GHB come in the bottom of the list, with approximately 4 percent of teens trying them.

In an attempt to learn when people were most likely to start using drugs, psychiatrists Kevin Chen and Denise B. Kandel of Columbia University followed 1,160 teens from adolescence to adulthood. Beginning in 1971 when the subjects were fifteen years old, and again at age twenty-five, twenty-nine, and thirty-five, the researchers interviewed the subjects about their drug use habits (including alcohol and tobacco). Chen and Kandel wrote in their 1995 study that the age period with the biggest risk was between sixteen and twenty; they found that those subjects who reached age twenty-one without using drugs were unlikely to do so later in life, and those who reached age twenty-nine without smoking or drinking alcohol continued to abstain throughout their lives.

Many researchers have documented reasons why teens try drugs. Teens may feel pressured by their friends to try drugs, they may have easy access to drugs, they may use drugs to rebel against their family or society, or they make take an illegal drug because they are curious about it or for the pleasurable feelings it gives them. Teens also take drugs to feel like an adult, for status among their peers, to lose their inhibitions, or simply because there is nothing else to do. Some teens—those who may live in an abusive home, feel unloved or unwanted, or have trouble in school—take drugs to forget the emotional pain they feel. Adolescent drug users may also be clinically depressed and take drugs to make them feel good or "normal." The Partnership Attitude Tracking Study found there is a real difference in personality types between teens who use and do not use marijuana. Marijuana users are more likely to be thrill seekers and risk takers who like to break the rules. Nonusers tend to be much more conservative than users; they value social approval, enjoy school, and are less likely to take risks.

Some researchers concentrate on who uses and is likely to use marijuana because of the belief that using marijuana leads to harder drug use. Others argue that some users are genetically predisposed to drug abuse and addiction, while many claim that environment is more a determinant of drug abuse. These issues and others are debated in the following chapter.

"Addiction is a brain disease expressed in the form of compulsive behavior."

Addiction Is a Brain Disease

Alan I. Leshner

Alan I. Leshner is the director of the National Institute on Drug Abuse at the National Institutes of Health. In the following viewpoint Leshner argues that while addiction begins with a voluntary action—ingesting drugs—it ends with long-lasting changes in the user's brain structure and function. These changes, he asserts, result in a brain disease that is responsible for the compulsion addicts feel to continue taking drugs. Addicts who give in to the uncontrollable and involuntary craving for drugs are not experiencing a failure of willpower but instead the expression of a brain disease.

As you read, consider the following questions:
1. Why is focusing on whether an addict suffers physical or psychological withdrawal symptoms a distraction from the real issues, in the author's opinion?
2. According to Leshner, why are repeated treatments for drug abuse necessary?
3. What is Leshner's response to those who wonder what happened to heroin addicts from thirty years ago?

Alan I. Leshner, "Addiction Is a Brain Disease," *Issues in Science and Technology*, vol. 17, Spring 2001, p. 75.

The United States is stuck in its drug abuse metaphors and in polarized arguments about them. Everyone has an opinion. One side insists that we must control supply, the other that we must reduce demand. People see addiction as either a disease or as a failure of will. None of this bumper-sticker analysis moves us forward. The truth is that we will make progress in dealing with drug issues only when our national discourse and our strategies are as complex and comprehensive as the problem itself.

An Evolving Concept

A core concept that has been evolving with scientific advances over the past decade is that drug addiction is a brain disease that develops over time as a result of the initially voluntary behavior of using drugs. The consequence is virtually uncontrollable compulsive drug craving, seeking, and use that interferes with, if not destroys, an individual's functioning in the family and in society. This medical condition demands formal treatment.

We now know in great detail the brain mechanisms through which drugs acutely modify mood, memory, perception, and emotional states. Using drugs repeatedly over time changes brain structure and function in fundamental and long-lasting ways that can persist long after the individual stops using them. Addiction comes about through an array of neuroadaptive changes and the laying down and strengthening of new memory connections in various circuits in the brain. We do not yet know all the relevant mechanisms, but the evidence suggests that those long-lasting brain changes are responsible for the distortions of cognitive and emotional functioning that characterize addicts, particularly including the compulsion to use drugs that is the essence of addiction. It is as if drugs have highjacked the brain's natural motivational control circuits, resulting in drug use becoming the sole, or at least the top, motivational priority for the individual. Thus, the majority of the biomedical community now considers addiction, in its essence, to be a brain disease: a condition caused by persistent changes in brain structure and function.

This brain-based view of addiction has generated substantial controversy, particularly among people who seem able to think only in polarized ways. Many people erroneously still believe that biological and behavioral explanations are alternative or competing ways to understand phenomena, when in fact they are complementary and integratable. Modern science has taught that it is much too simplistic to set biology in opposition to behavior or to pit willpower against brain chemistry. Addiction involves inseparable biological and behavioral components. It is the quintessential biobehavioral disorder.

Many people also erroneously still believe that drug addiction is simply a failure of will or of strength of character. Research contradicts that position. However, the recognition that addiction is a brain disease does not mean that the addict is simply a hapless victim. Addiction begins with the voluntary behavior of using drugs, and addicts must participate in and take some significant responsibility for their recovery. Thus, having this brain disease does not absolve the addict of responsibility for his or her behavior, but it does explain why an addict cannot simply stop using drugs by sheer force of will alone. It also dictates a much more sophisticated approach to dealing with the array of problems surrounding drug abuse and addiction in our society.

The Essence of Addiction

The entire concept of addiction has suffered greatly from imprecision and misconception. In fact, if it were possible, it would be best to start all over with some new, more neutral term. The confusion comes about in part because of a now archaic distinction between whether specific drugs are "physically" or "psychologically" addicting. The distinction historically revolved around whether or not dramatic physical withdrawal symptoms occur when an individual stops taking a drug; what we in the field now call "physical dependence."

However, 20 years of scientific research has taught that focusing on this physical versus psychological distinction is off the mark and a distraction from the real issues. From both clinical and policy perspectives, it actually does not matter very much what physical withdrawal symptoms occur. Physical dependence is not that important, because even the dramatic withdrawal symptoms of heroin and alcohol addiction can now be easily managed with appropriate medications. Even more important, many of the most dangerous and addicting drugs, including methamphetamine and crack cocaine, do not produce very severe physical dependence symptoms upon withdrawal.

What really matters most is whether or not a drug causes what we now know to be the essence of addiction: uncontrollable, compulsive drug craving, seeking, and use, even in the face of negative health and social consequences. This is the crux of how the Institute of Medicine, the American Psychiatric Association, and the American Medical Association define addiction and how we all should use the term. It is really only this compulsive quality of addiction that matters in the long run to the addict and to his or her family and that should matter to society as a whole. Compulsive craving that overwhelms all other motivations is the root cause of the massive health and social problems associated with drug addiction. In updating our national discourse on drug abuse, we should keep in mind this simple definition: Addiction is a brain disease expressed in the form of compulsive behavior. Both developing and recovering from it depend on biology, behavior, and social context.

Crossing a Threshold

It is also important to correct the common misimpression that drug use, abuse, and addiction are points on a single continuum along which one slides back and forth over time, moving from user to addict, then back to occasional user, then back to addict. Clinical observation and more formal research studies support the view that, once addicted, the individual has moved into a different state of being. It is as if a threshold has been crossed. Very few people appear able to successfully return to occasional use after having been truly addicted. Unfortunately, we do not yet have a clear biological or behavioral marker of that transition from voluntary drug use to addiction. However, a body of scientific evidence is rapidly developing that points to an array of cellular and molecular changes in specific brain circuits. Moreover, many of these brain changes are common to all chemical addictions, and some also are typical of other compulsive behaviors such as pathological overeating.

Addiction should be understood as a chronic recurring illness. Although some addicts do gain full control over their drug use after a single treatment episode, many have relapses. Repeated treatments become necessary to increase the intervals between and diminish the intensity of relapses, until the individual achieves abstinence.

The complexity of this brain disease is not atypical, because virtually no brain diseases are simply biological in nature and expression. All, including stroke, Alzheimer's disease, schizophrenia, and clinical depression, include some behavioral and social aspects. What may make addiction seem unique among brain diseases, however, is that it does begin with a clearly voluntary behavior—the initial decision to use drugs. Moreover, not everyone who ever uses drugs goes on to become addicted. Individuals differ substantially in how easily and quickly they become addicted and in their preferences for particular substances. Consistent with the biobehavioral nature of addiction, these individual differences result from a combination of environmental and biological, particularly genetic, factors. In fact, estimates are that between 50 and 70 percent of the variability in susceptibility to becoming addicted can be accounted for by genetic factors.

Uncontrollable Behavior

Over time the addict loses substantial control over his or her initially voluntary behavior, and it becomes compulsive. For many people these behaviors are truly uncontrollable, just like the behavioral expression of any other brain disease. Schizophrenics cannot control their hallucinations and delusions. Parkinson's patients cannot control their trembling. Clinically depressed patients cannot voluntarily control their moods. Thus, once one is addicted, the characteristics of the illness—and the treatment approaches—are not that different from most other brain diseases. No matter how one develops an illness, once one has it, one is in the diseased state and needs treatment.

Moreover, voluntary behavior patterns are, of course, involved in the etiology and progression of many other illnesses, albeit not all brain diseases. Examples abound, including hypertension, arteriosclerosis and other cardiovascular diseases, diabetes, and forms of cancer in which the onset is heavily influenced by the individual's eating, exercise, smoking, and other behaviors.

Drugs and Brain Chemicals

The discovery of the endorphins (the brain's own opiates) in the 1970s brought home the possibility that drugs may compensate for an inborn or acquired chemical deficiency. These endorphins are chemical messengers made in nervous tissue and released in response to painful, frightening, or satisfying experiences (e.g. sexual intercourse). They turn off aversive (unpleasant) messages and mediate reward. Intuitively, it is highly desirable to have an abundant supply at your disposal. If you are deficient in endorphins and happen to be exposed to opioids, or short of dopamine and exposed to amphetamine, it seems logical to suppose that you will be particularly sensitive to the rewarding or aversion-reducing effect. We know from research into depression that people can be naturally low in certain chemical messengers (for example, serotonin), and that this may increase their susceptibility to suicide. Perhaps this deficiency could be genetically programmed, an idea which finds some support in animal experiments. This finding has prompted the suggestion that some addicts may be no more to blame for their state than diabetics. Just as a diabetic needs insulin to maintain normal functioning, perhaps the endorphin-deficient junkie needs heroin and the dopamine-starved cocaine snorter must have his stimulant.

Philip Robson, *Forbidden Drugs*, 1999.

Addictive behaviors do have special characteristics related to the social contexts in which they originate. All of the environmental cues surrounding initial drug use and development of the addiction actually become "conditioned" to that drug use and are thus critical to the development and expression of addiction. Environmental cues are paired in time with an individual's initial drug use experiences and, through classical conditioning, take on conditioned stimulus properties. When those cues are present at a later time, they elicit anticipation of a drug experience and thus generate tremendous drug craving. Cue-induced craving is one of the most frequent causes of drug use relapses, even after long periods of abstinence, independently of whether drugs are available.

The salience of environmental or contextual cues helps explain why reentry to one's community can be so difficult for addicts leaving the controlled environments of treatment or correctional settings and why aftercare is so essential to successful recovery. The person who became addicted in the home environment is constantly exposed to the cues conditioned to his or her initial drug use, such as the neighborhood where he or she hung out, drug-using buddies, or the lamppost where he or she bought drugs. Simple exposure to those cues automatically triggers craving and can lead rapidly to relapses. This is one reason why someone who apparently overcame drug cravings while in prison or residential treatment could quickly revert to drug use upon returning home. In fact, one of the major goals of drug addiction treatment is to teach addicts how to deal with the cravings caused by inevitable exposure to these conditioned cues.

Implications

Understanding addiction as a brain disease has broad and significant implications for the public perception of addicts and their families, for addiction treatment practice, and for some aspects of public policy. On the other hand, this biomedical view of addiction does not speak directly to and is unlikely to bear significantly on many other issues, including specific strategies for controlling the supply of drugs and whether initial drug use should be legal or not. Moreover, the brain disease model of addiction does not address the question of whether specific drugs of abuse can also be potential medicines. Examples abound of drugs that can be both highly addicting and extremely effective medicines. The best-known example is the appropriate use of morphine as a treatment for pain. Nevertheless, a number of practical lessons can be drawn from the scientific understanding of addiction.

It is no wonder addicts cannot simply quit on their own. They have an illness that requires biomedical treatment. People often assume that because addiction begins with a voluntary behavior and is expressed in the form of excess behavior, people should just be able to quit by force of will alone. However, it is essential to understand when dealing with addicts that we are dealing with individuals whose brains have been altered by drug use. They need drug addiction treatment. We know that, contrary to common belief, very few addicts actually do just stop on their own. Observing that there are very few heroin addicts in their 50 or 60s, people frequently ask what happened to those who were heroin addicts 30 years ago, assuming that they must have quit on their own. However, longitudinal studies find that only a very small fraction actually quit on their own. The rest have either been successfully treated, are currently in maintenance treatment, or (for about half) are dead. Consider the example of smoking cigarettes: Various studies have found that between 3 and 7 percent of people who try to quit on their own each year actually succeed. Science has at last convinced the public that depression is not just a lot of sadness; that depressed individuals are in a different brain state and thus require treatment to get their symptoms under control. The same is true for schizophrenic patients. It is time to recognize that this is also the case for addicts.

Personal Responsibility

The role of personal responsibility is undiminished but clarified. Does having a brain disease mean that people who are addicted no longer have any responsibility for their behavior or that they are simply victims of their own genetics and brain chemistry? Of course not. Addiction begins with the voluntary behavior of drug use, and although genetic characteristics may predispose individuals to be more or less susceptible to becoming addicted, genes do not doom one to become an addict. This is one major reason why efforts to prevent drug use are so vital to any comprehensive strategy to deal with the nation's drug problems. Initial drug use is a voluntary, and therefore preventable, behavior.

Moreover, as with any illness, behavior becomes a critical part of recovery. At a minimum, one must comply with the treatment regimen, which is harder than it sounds. Treatment compliance is the biggest cause of relapses for all chronic illnesses, including asthma, diabetes, hypertension, and addiction. Moreover, treatment compliance rates are no worse for addiction than for these other illnesses, ranging from 30 to 50 percent. Thus, for drug addiction as well as for other chronic diseases, the individual's motivation and behavior are clearly important parts of success in treatment and recovery.

Implications for Treatment Approaches and Treatment Expectations

Maintaining this comprehensive biobehavioral understanding of addiction also speaks to what needs to be provided in drug treatment programs. Again, we must be careful not to pit biology against behavior. The National Institute on Drug Abuse's *Principles of Effective Drug Addiction Treatment* provides a detailed discussion of how we must treat all aspects of the individual, not just the biological component or the behavioral component. As with other brain diseases such as schizophrenia and depression, the data show that the best drug addiction treatment approaches attend to the entire individual, combining the use of medications, behavioral therapies, and attention to necessary social services and rehabilitation. These might include such services as family therapy to enable the patient to return to successful family life, mental health services, education and vocational training, and housing services.

That does not mean, of course, that all individuals need all components of treatment and all rehabilitation services. Another principle of effective addiction treatment is that the array of services included in an individual's treatment plan must be matched to his or her particular set of needs. Moreover, since those needs will surely change over the course of recovery, the array of services provided will need to be continually reassessed and adjusted. . . .

Addicts Need Compassion

The message from the now very broad and deep array of scientific evidence is absolutely clear. If we as a society ever hope to make any real progress in dealing with our drug problems, we are going to have to rise above moral outrage that addicts have "done it to themselves" and develop strategies that are as sophisticated and as complex as the problem itself. Whether addicts are "victims" or not, once addicted they must be seen as "brain disease patients."

Moreover, although our national traditions do argue for compassion for those who are sick, no matter how they contracted their illnesses, I recognize that many addicts have disrupted not only their own lives but those of their families and their broader communities, and thus do not easily generate compassion. However, no matter how one may feel about addicts and their behavioral histories, an extensive body of scientific evidence shows that approaching addiction as a treatable illness is extremely cost-effective, both financially and in terms of broader societal impacts such as family violence, crime, and other forms of social upheaval. Thus, it is clearly in everyone's interest to get past the hurt and indignation and slow the drain of drugs on society by enhancing drug use prevention efforts and providing treatment to all who need it.

"A simple test of a true physical disease is whether it can be shown to exist in a corpse. There are no bodily signs of addiction itself (as opposed to its effects) that can be identified in a dead body."

Addiction Is Not a Brain Disease

Jeffrey A. Schaler

Jeffrey A. Schaler, a psychologist specializing in addiction, is the author of several books on drug abuse, including *Addiction Is a Choice*, from which this viewpoint is excerpted. Schaler contends that addiction is not a disease because it leaves no physical evidence in the human body. The effects of addiction may cause diseases—such as cirrhosis of the liver or lung cancer—but this does not prove that drinking or smoking too much are themselves diseases. Schaler concludes that people abuse drugs, alcohol, and tobacco because they choose to.

As you read, consider the following questions:
1. Why is the view that drug addiction is a disease so prevalent, in Schaler's opinion?
2. What is nosology, as defined by the author?
3. What is the difference between a symptom and a sign, and which is used most often in making a diagnosis, as explained by the author?

If you watch TV, read the newspaper, or listen to almost any social worker or religious minister, you soon pick up the idea that addiction is a condition in which addicts just physically cannot control themselves, and that this condition is a medical disease.

The federal government views alcohol addiction as a disease characterized by *loss of control*, with a physiological 'etiology' (cause) independent of volition. According to a typical statement of the government's view by Otis R. Bowen, former secretary of health and human services,

> millions of children have a genetic predisposition to alcoholism . . . alcohol use by young people has been found to be a 'gateway' drug preceding other drug use . . . about 1 out of every 15 kids will eventually become an alcoholic. . . . Alcoholism is a disease, and this disease is highly treatable.

You may easily conclude that all the experts agree with this kind of thinking. Most people with no special interest in the subject probably never get to hear another point of view.

Differing Opinions

The true situation is a bit more complicated. Public opinion overwhelmingly accepts the claim that addiction is a disease, but the general public's views are seriously inconsistent. A 1987 study of public views on alcoholism showed that over 85 percent of people believe that alcoholism is a disease, but most of them also believe things that contradict the disease theory. Many people seem to support and reject the disease theory at the same time. For instance, they often say they believe that alcoholism is a disease and also that it is a sign of moral weakness.

The addiction treatment providers, the many thousands of people who make their living in the addiction treatment industry, mostly accept the disease theory. They are, in fact, for the most part, 'recovered addicts' themselves, redeemed sinners who spend their lives being paid to preach the gospel that social deviants are sick.

Among those psychologists and others who think, write, discuss, and conduct research in this area, however, opinion is much more divided. In this small world, there is an ongoing battle between the 'disease model' and the 'free-will model'.

Biomedical and psychosocial scientists range across both sides of the controversy. Some biomedical researchers accept the disease model and assert that genetic and physiological differences account for alcoholism. Other biomedical researchers have investigated their claims and pronounced them invalid. Many social scientists reject the idea that alcoholics or other addicts constitute a homogeneous group. They hold that individual differences, personal values, expectations, and environmental factors are key correlates to heavy drinking and drug-taking. Others reject strictly psychological theories. Some sociologists regard the disease model of alcoholism as a human construction based on desire for social control. Some embrace the disease model even while agreeing that addiction may not be a real disease—they hold that utility warrants labeling it as such. Their opponents believe the disease model does more harm than good. . . .

What Is a Disease?

Is addiction really a disease? Let's clarify a few matters. The classification of behavior as socially unacceptable does not prove its label as a disease. Adherents of the disease model sometimes respond to the claim that addiction is not a disease by emphasizing the terrible problems people create as a result of their addictions, but that is entirely beside the point. The fact that some behavior has horrible consequences does not show that it's a disease.

The 'success' of 'treatment programs' run by people who view addiction as a disease would not demonstrate that addiction was a disease—any more than the success of other religious groups in converting people from vicious practices would prove the theological tenets of these religious groups. However, this possibility need not concern us, since all known treatment programs are, in fact, ineffective.

I will not go into the claims of a genetic basis for 'alcoholism' or other addictions. A genetic predisposition toward some kind of behavior, say, speaking in tongues, would not show that those with the predisposition had a disease. Variations in skin and eye color, for example, are genetically determined, but are not diseases. Fair-skinned people sunburn easily. The fairness of their skin is genetically determined, yet their susceptibility to sunburn is not considered a disease. Neither would a genetic predisposition toward some kind of behavior necessarily show that the predisposed persons could not consciously change their behavior.

Not Helpless Victims

The fact that many, perhaps most, addicts are in control of their actions and appetites for circumscribed periods of time shows that they are not perpetually helpless victims of a chronic disease. They are instigators of their addiction, just as they are agents of their own recovery . . . or nonrecovery. The potential for self-control should allow society to endorse expectations and demands of addicts that would never be made of someone with a true involuntary illness. Making such demands is, of course, no assurance that they'll be met. But confidence in their very legitimacy would encourage a range of policy and therapeutic options—using consequences and coercion—that is incompatible with the idea of a no-fault brain disease.

Efforts to neutralize the stigma of addiction by convincing the public that the addict has a "brain disease" are understandable, but in the long run they have no more likelihood of success than the use of feel-good slogans to help a child acquire "self-esteem." Neither respectability nor a sense of self-worth can be bestowed; both must be earned. The best way for any institution, politician, or advocate to combat the stigma of addiction is to promote conditions—both within treatment settings and in society at large—that help the addict develop self-discipline and, along with it, self-respect. In this way, former addicts become visible symbols of hard work, responsibility, and lawfulness—potent antidotes to stigma.

Sally Satel, *Drug Addiction and Drug Policy: The Struggle to Control Dependence*, 2001.

With so much commonsense evidence to refute it, why is the view of drug addiction as a disease so prevalent? Incredible as it may seem, because doctors say so. A leading alcoholism researcher once asserted that alcoholism is a disease simply because people go to doctors for it. Undoubtedly, drug 'addicts' seek help from doctors for two reasons. Many addicts have a significant psychological investment in maintaining this view, having been told, and come to believe, that their eventual recovery depends on believing they have a disease. They may even have come to accept that they will die if they question the disease model of addiction. And treatment professionals have a significant economic investment at stake. The more behaviors are diagnosed as diseases, the more they will be paid by health insurance companies for 'treating' these diseases.

When we consider whether drug addiction is a disease we are concerned with what causes the drug to get *into* the body. It's quite irrelevant what the drug does *after* it's in the body. I certainly don't for a moment doubt that the taking of many drugs *causes* disease. Prolonged heavy drinking of alcoholic beverages can cause cirrhosis of the liver. Prolonged smoking of cigarettes somewhat raises the risk of various diseases such as lung cancer. But this uncontroversial fact is quite distinct from any claim that the activity is itself a disease.

Some doctors make a specialty of occupation-linked disorders. For example, there is a pattern of lung and other diseases associated with working down a coal mine. But this does not show that mining coal is itself a disease. Other enterprising physicians specialize in treating diseases arising from sports: there is a pattern of diseases resulting from swimming, another from football, yet another from long-distance running. This does not demonstrate that these sports, or the inclination to pursue these sports, are themselves diseases. So, for instance, the fact that a doctor may be exceptionally knowledgeable about the effects of alcohol on the body, and may therefore be accepted as an expert on 'alcoholism', does nothing to show that alcoholism itself is a legitimate medical concept.

Addiction, a Physical Disease?

If addiction is a disease, then presumably it's either a bodily or a mental disease. What criteria might justify defining addiction as a physical illness? Pathologists use nosology—the classification of diseases—to select, from among the phenomena they study, those that qualify as true diseases. Diseases are listed in standard pathology textbooks because they meet the nosological criteria for disease classification. A simple test of a true physical disease is whether it can be shown to exist in a corpse. There are no bodily signs of addiction itself (as opposed to its effects) that can be identified in a dead body. Addiction is therefore not listed in standard pathology textbooks.

Pathology, as revolutionized by Rudolf Virchow (1821–1902), requires an identifiable alteration in bodily tissue, a change in the cells of the body, for disease classification. No such identifiable pathology has been found in the bodies of heavy drinkers and drug users. This alone justifies the view that addiction is not a physical disease.

A symptom is subjective evidence from the patient: the patient reports certain pains and other sensations. A sign is something that can be identified in the patient's body, irrespective of the patient's reported experiences. In standard medical practice, the diagnosis of disease can be based on signs alone or on a combination of signs and symptoms, but only rarely on symptoms alone. A sign is objective physical evidence such as a lesion or chemical imbalance. Signs may be found through medical tests.

Sometimes a routine physical examination reveals signs of disease when no symptoms are reported. In such cases the disease is said to be 'asymptomatic'—without symptoms. For example, sugar in the urine combined with other signs may lead to a diagnosis of asymptomatic diabetes. Such a diagnosis is made solely on the basis of signs. It is inconceivable that addiction could ever be diagnosed on the basis of bodily signs alone. (The *effects* of heavy alcohol consumption can of course be inferred from bodily signs, but that, remember, is a different matter.) To speak of 'asymptomatic addiction' would be absurd. . . .

We continually hear that 'addiction is a disease just like diabetes'. Yet there is no such thing as asymptomatic addiction, and *logically there could not be*. Moreover, the analogy cannot be turned around. It would be awkward to tell a person with diabetes that his condition was 'just like addiction' and inaccurate too: When a person with diabetes is deprived of insulin he will suffer and in severe cases may even die. When a heavy drinker or other drug user is deprived of alcohol or other drugs his physical health most often improves.

Mental illnesses are diagnosed on the basis of symptoms, not signs. Perhaps, then, addiction is a mental illness, a psychiatric disease. Where does it fit into the scheme of psychiatric disorders?

Psychiatric disorders can be categorized in three groups: organic disorders, functional disorders, and antisocial behavior. Organic disorders include various forms of dementia such as those caused by HIV-1 infection, acute alcohol intoxication, brain tumor or injury, dementia of the Alzheimer's type, general paresis, and multi-infarct dementia. These are physical diseases with identifiable bodily signs. Addiction has no such identifiable signs.

Functional disorders include fears (anxiety disorders), discouragements (mood disorders), and stupidities (cognitive disorders). These are mental in the sense that they involve mental activities. As [Thomas] Szasz has pointed out, they are diseases "only in a metaphorical sense."

Forms of antisocial behavior categorized as psychiatric illness include crime, suicide, personality disorders, and maladaptive and maladjusted behavior. Some people consider these 'disorders' because they vary from the norm and involve danger to self or others. According to Szasz, however, they are "neither 'mental' nor 'diseases.'" If addiction qualifies as an antisocial behavior, this does not necessarily imply that it is mental or a disease.

Addiction is not listed in the American Psychiatric Association's Diagnostic and Statistical Manual of Mental Disorders IV (DSM-IV). What was once listed as alcoholism is now referred to as alcohol dependence and abuse. These are listed under the category of substance-related disorders. They would not fit the category of organic disorders because they are described in terms of behavior only. They would conceivably fit the functional disorder category but probably would be subordinated to one of the established disorders such as discouragement or anxiety.

Thus, it's difficult to classify addiction as either a physical or a mental disease. . . .

The term 'alcoholism' has become so loaded with prescriptive intent that it no longer describes any drinking behavior accurately and should be abandoned. 'Heavy drinking' is a more descriptive term. It is imprecise, but so is 'alcoholism'.

If we continue to use the term 'alcoholism', however, we

should bear in mind that there is no precisely defined condition, activity, or entity called alcoholism in the way there is a precise condition known as lymphosarcoma of the mesenteric glands, for example. The actual usage of the term 'alcoholism', like 'addiction', has become primarily normative and prescriptive: a derogatory, stigmatizing word applied to people who drink 'too much'. The definition of 'too much' depends on the values of the speaker, which may be different from those of the person doing the drinking.

Calling addiction a 'disease' tells us more about the labeler than the labelee. Diseases are medical conditions. They can be discovered on the basis of bodily signs. They are something people have. They are involuntary. For example, the disease of syphilis was discovered. It is identified by specific signs. It is not a form of activity and is not based in human values. While certain behaviors increase the likelihood of acquiring syphilis, and while the acquisition of syphilis has consequences for subsequent social interaction, the behavior and the disease are separate phenomena. Syphilis meets the nosological criteria for disease classification in a pathology textbook. Unlike addiction, syphilis is a disease that can be diagnosed in a corpse.

Once we recognize that addiction cannot be classified as a literal disease, its nature as an ethical choice becomes clearer. A person starts, moderates, or abstains from drinking because that person wants to. People do the same thing with heroin, cocaine, and tobacco. Such choices reflect the person's values. The person, a moral agent, chooses to use drugs or refrains from using drugs because he or she finds meaning in doing so.

"The more often you use marijuana, the more likely you will use cocaine and heroin."

Marijuana Use Leads to the Use of Other Drugs

Jim McDonough

In 2002 the RAND Institute's Drug Research Policy Center sponsored a study examining the "gateway theory," which postulates that marijuana use leads to the abuse of other drugs such as cocaine and heroin. In the following viewpoint Jim McDonough argues that the media has misrepresented the results of the study by claiming that it found that marijuana is not a gateway drug. In fact, McDonough contends, the study's researchers discovered that the correlation between marijuana use and other drug use is high, and that users who abuse marijuana on a frequent basis are more likely to use cocaine and heroin. McDonough is the director of the Florida Office of Drug Control and formerly served as director of strategic planning at the Office of National Drug Control Policy.

As you read, consider the following questions:
1. What previous study results are accepted by the author of the RAND study, according to McDonough?
2. What is the "common factor" theory, as cited by the author?
3. What are the RAND study's important findings that were missed by the press and promarijuana lobby, according to McDonough?

Jim McDonough, "A Weed by Any Other Name Smells the Same," *Christian Science Monitor*, December 16, 2002, p. 9. Copyright © 2002 by Jim McDonough. Reproduced by permission.

B ig excitement has hit the drug legalization world. A [2002] RAND Drug Policy Research Center study reported that marijuana may look, act, and smell like a gateway drug to abuse of harder drugs, but that possibly it is not a gateway drug after all.

A Misrepresented Study

The marijuana normalizers—as in, "let's make marijuana use normal, or acceptable"—loved it; so did some of the press. Both were quick to misportray the study, so much so that the author of the study himself was dismayed.

Andrew Morral of RAND believes he did everything he could to explain he did not disprove the gateway theory but, as he told me, "The story about it misrepresented both our findings and my comments about the relevance of our findings to US drug policy. RAND and I have taken pains to emphasize that we do not believe we have disproved the gateway theory."

The study did say that a high incidence of progression from marijuana to heroin and cocaine use is apparent; that the younger you are when you start using marijuana, the more likely you are to end up using cocaine and heroin; that the more often you use marijuana, the more likely you will use cocaine and heroin.

In short, the study shows the correlation between marijuana and other drug abuse to be high.

Indeed, the study accepts previous studies that have demonstrated the probability that heroin and cocaine use increases 85 times for marijuana users when compared with those who are not marijuana users; that early teen use of marijuana is even more highly correlated with other drug use than late teen marijuana use; and that the more puffs of marijuana you take, the more likely you move on to injections and snorting of even more dangerous drugs.

But here's where the misunderstanding begins. The study says that maybe these terrible things happen because the people who use all these nasty drugs do it because they have a propensity for drug use, and marijuana is the first illegal drug to present itself to the young.

Dr. Morral calls that the "common factor" theory.

In other words, all drug users like all drugs; marijuana just comes along first. He suggests that this theory might be more accurate than the gateway theory.

Marijuana Puts Teens at Greater Risk

Teens who drank and smoked cigarettes at least once in the past month are 30 times more likely to smoke marijuana than those who didn't. Teens who drank, smoked cigarettes, and used marijuana at least once in the past month are more than 16 times as likely to use another drug like cocaine, heroin or LSD. . . .

The point for parents and teens is that those youngsters who smoke pot are at vastly greater risk of moving on to harder drugs. [The National Center on Addiction and Substance Abuse's] studies reveal that the younger and more often a teen smokes pot, the more likely that teen is to use cocaine. A child who uses marijuana before age 12 is 42 times more likely to use cocaine, heroin or other drugs than one who first smokes pot after age 16.

Joseph A. Califano, *Wall Street Journal*, March 26, 1999.

But is a gateway not a gateway because it happens to present itself in front of where you want to go?

Perhaps this study's findings appear trivial. They aren't. If marijuana is merely the door through which those inclined to use drugs pass because it is convenient, all the more reason to keep that door locked.

Marijuana Is Dangerous

I'm convinced that's the best way to view Morral's findings, because the pro-marijuana lobby and much of what the press missed in this study, as well as other careful studies, were findings that suggest:

• There is a strong correlation between marijuana and other drug abuse, with marijuana almost always occurring first.

• Marijuana, all by itself, is a dangerous drug.

• There is a strong correlation between marijuana use and schizophrenia.

• Marijuana itself is addictive.

• Youth marijuana use correlates highly with violence, truancy, and other behavioral problems.

• The younger the marijuana user, the more psychological and physiological damage done, and the more likely that other drugs will follow.

• Smoking three marijuana joints a day can cause the equivalent respiratory damage associated with 20 cigarettes a day. Marijuana smokers show significantly more respiratory symptoms than people who don't smoke it.

• Prolonged use can cause attention deficit and deterioration in memory.

Over the years, I have talked with hundreds of addicts and treatment counselors. They say that marijuana was virtually always the beginning of a long, ugly journey; that marijuana is the most insidious of the illegal drugs because of the seductive, but often wrong, rationale that you can quit any time you want; that easy access to marijuana is a major part of the problem; and that their lives would have been far better if marijuana had been out of the picture.

As we do more studies, we might turn to these people for insight.

So what of the utility of the "common factor" theory over the "gateway" theory? A weed by any other name still smells the same.

"Those who use drugs may have an underlying propensity to do so that is not specific to any one drug."

Marijuana Use May Not Lead to the Use of Other Drugs

Drug Policy Research Center

Many people believe that marijuana is a "gateway" drug—that its use results in a user being more likely to abuse harder drugs such as cocaine and heroin. The following viewpoint summarizes the 2002 RAND Institute's Drug Policy Research Center (DPRC) report, which examines drug use patterns in order to determine the validity of the gateway theory. While the results do not disprove the gateway theory, the report's authors found that other factors could explain the correlation between marijuana use and other drug use. The researchers concluded that some individuals may have a propensity for using drugs, and marijuana is simply the first drug that becomes available to them.

As you read, consider the following questions:

1. What three facts do the authors list to support the gateway theory?
2. What is the "common factor" theory, as explained by the report's authors?
3. According to the authors, how many marijuana arrests are made each year in the United States?

M arijuana is widely regarded as a "gateway" drug, that is, one whose use results in an increased likelihood of using more serious drugs such as cocaine and heroin. This gateway effect is one of the principal reasons cited in defense of laws prohibiting the use or possession of marijuana. A [2002] analysis by RAND's Drug Policy Research Center (DPRC) suggests that data typically used to support a marijuana gateway effect can be explained as well by a different theory. The new research, by Andrew Morral, associate director of RAND Public Safety and Justice, Daniel McCaffrey, and Susan Paddock, has implications for U.S. marijuana policy. However, decisions about relaxing U.S. marijuana laws must necessarily take into account many other factors in addition to whether or not marijuana is a gateway drug.

Support for the Gateway Effect

Although marijuana has never been shown to have a gateway effect, three drug initiation facts support the notion that marijuana use raises the risk of hard-drug use:

- Marijuana users are many times more likely than nonusers to progress to hard-drug use.
- Almost all who have used both marijuana and hard drugs used marijuana first.
- The greater the frequency of marijuana use, the greater the likelihood of using hard drugs later.

This evidence would appear to make a strong case for a gateway effect. However, another explanation has been suggested: Those who use drugs may have an underlying propensity to do so that is not specific to any one drug. There is some support for such a "common-factor" model in studies of genetic, familial, and environmental factors influencing drug use. The presence of a common propensity could explain why people who use one drug are so much more likely to use another than are people who do not use the first drug. It has also been suggested that marijuana use precedes hard-drug use simply because opportunities to use marijuana come earlier in life than opportunities to use hard drugs. The DPRC analysis offers the first quantitative evidence that these observations can, without resort to a gateway effect, explain the strong observed associations between marijuana and hard-drug initiation.

The DPRC research team examined the drug use patterns reported by more than 58,000 U.S. residents between the ages of 12 and 25 who participated in the National Household Surveys on Drug Abuse (NHSDA) conducted between 1982 and 1994. Using a statistical model, the researchers tested whether the observed patterns of drug use initiation might be expected if drug initiation risks were determined exclusively by

- when youths had a first opportunity to use each drug
- individuals' drug use propensity, which was assumed to be normally distributed in the population
- chance (or random) factors.

To put it another way, the researchers addressed the question: Could the drug initiation facts listed in the first section of this brief be explained without recourse to a marijuana gateway effect?

The research team found that these associations could be explained without any gateway effects:

- The statistical model could explain the increased risk of hard-drug initiation experienced by marijuana users. Indeed, the model predicted that marijuana users would be at even greater risk of drug use progression than the actual NHSDA data shown (see Figure 1).
- The model predicted that only a fraction of hard-drug

Figure 1. Probabilities of Initiating Hard Drugs, Marijuana Users and Nonusers

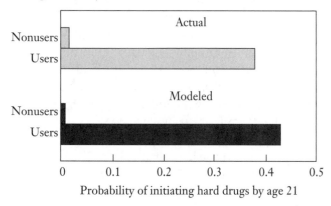

users would not have tried marijuana first. Whereas in the NHSDA data 1.6 percent of adolescents tried hard drugs before marijuana, the model predicted an even stronger sequencing of initiation, with just 1.1 percent trying hard drugs first.

• The modeled relationship between marijuana use frequency and hard-drug initiation could closely match the actual relationship (see Figure 2).

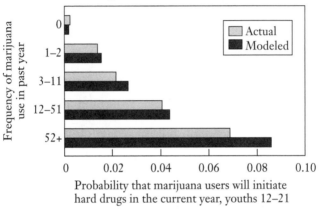

Figure 2. Probabilities of Hard-Drug Initiation, Given Marijuana Use Frequency in the Preceding Year

Probability that marijuana users will initiate hard drugs in the current year, youths 12–21

The new DPRC research thus demonstrates that the phenomena supporting claims that marijuana is a gateway drug also support the alternative explanation: that it is not marijuana use but individuals' opportunities and unique propensities to use drugs that determine their risk of initiating hard drugs. The research does not disprove the gateway theory; it merely shows that another explanation is plausible.

Some might argue that as long as the gateway theory remains a possible explanation, policymakers should play it safe and retain current strictures against marijuana use and possession. That attitude might be a sound one if current marijuana policies were free of costs and harms. But prohibition policies are not cost-free, and their harms are significant: The more than 700,000 marijuana arrests per year in the United States burden individuals, families, neighborhoods, and society as a whole.

Marijuana policies should weigh these harms of prohibition against the harms of increased marijuana availability and use, harms that could include adverse effects on the health, development, education, and cognitive functioning of marijuana users. However, the harms of marijuana use can no longer be viewed as necessarily including an expansion of hard-drug use and its associated harms. This shift in perspective ought to change the overall balance between the harms and benefits of different marijuana policies. Whether it is sufficient to change it decisively is something that the new DPRC research cannot aid in resolving.

Periodical Bibliography

The following articles have been selected to supplement the diverse views presented in this chapter.

Mike Allen et al.

"Comparing the Influence of Parents and Peers on the Choice to Use Drugs: A Meta-Analytic Summary of the Literature," *Criminal Justice and Behavior*, April 2003.

Scott Baldauf

"When Parents Are a Part of the Drug Problem," *Christian Science Monitor*, August 28, 2000.

Lewis Beale

"When Stars Get Depressed," *Us*, March 31, 2003.

Richard J. Bonnie

"Addiction and Responsibility," *Social Research*, Fall 2001.

Joseph A. Califano Jr.

"It's All in the Family," *America*, January 15, 2000.

Economist

"Having It All: Cocaine Addiction," January 26, 2002.

Siobhan Gorman

"Why They Don't Just Say No," *National Journal*, August 18, 2001.

John H. Halpern

"Addiction Is a Disease," *Psychiatric Times*, October 2002.

Susan Kirsebbaum

"Darling, Pass the Xanax," *Harper's Bazaar*, May 2002.

Sandra Levy

"Beware the Dark Side of Pharmacy Life," *Drug Topics*, July 1, 2002.

Ernest P. Noble

"Addiction May Be in the Genes," *Los Angeles Times*, December 4, 2000.

Sally Satel

"Drugs: A Decision, Not a Disease," *Wall Street Journal*, April 27, 2001.

David Taylor

"Drugs on the Brain," *Meanjin*, June 2002.

Julia VanTine

"Hands-On Parenting Cuts Teen Drug Use," *Prevention*, August 2001.

Brian Vastag

"Boomers Don't Raise Potheads," *Journal of the American Medical Association*, September 19, 2001.

CHAPTER 3

Should Drug Testing Be Used?

Chapter Preface

The U.S. Supreme Court has long recognized that testing a person's blood or urine for signs of drug or alcohol use is a search under the Fourth Amendment. However, the Court has gradually been changing the rules about who may be legally tested and under what circumstances. Drug tests were first allowed if there was a suspicion that drug use may have caused an employee to have an accident on the job. But in the last fifteen years, the Court has also permitted random and suspicionless drug testing.

In 1989 the Supreme Court ruled on its first case involving drug testing. At issue in *Skinner v. Railway Labor Executives' Association* was a regulation that required drug and alcohol testing for railroad employees who were involved in accidents or who broke specified safety rules. The Court found that the government had a compelling interest in protecting the public's safety by ensuring that railroad employees were not impaired by drugs or alcohol. In this case, the Court ruled, the public's safety overrode the employees' right to privacy.

Also in 1989, the Supreme Court decided *National Treasury Employees Union v. Von Raab*. The Court upheld a U.S. Treasury regulation that required drug tests for employees directly involved in drug interdiction and enforcement and for those required to carry weapons. Protecting the public from the use of deadly force by customs agents who may be under the influence of drugs or alcohol also outweighed the employees' right to privacy, the Court ruled.

The next drug-testing case heard by the Supreme Court was *Vernonia School District 47J v. Acton* in 1995. The Vernonia School District claimed that there was widespread drug use in its schools, especially by its student athletes. Because high school athletes were considered role models by many students and because many were leaders of the schools' drug culture, the school district began random drug testing of all students participating in athletics. The Supreme Court upheld the district's testing requirement, writing that schools have many "responsibilities . . . as guardian and tutor of children entrusted to their care." In addition, it noted that students—especially those involved in sports who must change and shower in communal locker rooms—do not have as great an expectation of privacy as the general population. Because of the special needs of the school district to keep its student-athletes drug free, the Court found that the invasion of privacy in this case was justified.

The Court's next decision on drug testing was in 1997. It ruled that Georgia's law requiring political candidates to submit to and pass a drug test was unconstitutional. In *Chandler v. Miller*, the Court asserted that there was no evidence of a drug problem among Georgia's politicians, nor any special need—unlike in *Skinner*, *Von Raab*, or *Vernonia*—to ensure that the test takers were drug free. In this case, the drug-testing regulation was simply symbolic and served no public need.

In 2001 the Supreme Court overturned another drug-testing program. The Medical University of South Carolina had been testing pregnant women suspected of abusing drugs and giving the results of those who tested positive to the police. The women were then given the choice to either enter a treatment program or be prosecuted on drug charges. In *Ferguson v. City of Charleston*, the Supreme Court ruled that the testing was a gross violation of the women's right to privacy and that the hospital had no special need to justify the tests. Therefore, the testing was unconstitutional.

The last case heard by the Supreme Court was *Board of Education v. Earls* in 2002. At issue in this case was the school district's policy of requiring random drug tests of students who participated in extracurricular activities. Although the Court admitted that students who sang in the choir were in little danger of injury and did not use communal locker rooms and therefore did not have a lessened expectation of privacy, it upheld the random drug testing. The Court reasoned that the school district's interest in preventing drug use among its students outweighed the students' right to privacy.

The conflicting opinions about whether drug testing is necessary, constitutional, and effective are among the issues examined in this chapter.

"The drug testing of . . . students who participate in extracurricular activities effectively serves the School District's interest in protecting the safety and health of its students."

Testing Students for Drug Use Is Reasonable

Clarence Thomas

The following viewpoint is an excerpt from the Supreme Court opinion in *Board of Education v. Earls*, in which the Court ruled that school districts can test students who participate in extracurricular activities for illegal drug use. Justice Clarence Thomas argues that it is constitutional and perfectly reasonable for school districts to require students to undergo a drug test in order to combat the scourge of illegal drug use. Indeed, schools have a custodial responsibility toward students, he asserts. Moreover, according to Thomas, collecting urine samples is a negligible intrusion on students' privacy.

As you read, consider the following questions:
1. Why is a student's privacy interest limited in a public school environment, according to the Supreme Court?
2. Why is the method of urine collection even less problematic than it was in the *Vernonia* case, in Thomas's opinion?
3. What is the only consequence of a failed drug test in the Tecumseh School District, as cited by Thomas?

Clarence Thomas, *Board of Education of Independent School District No. 92 of Pottawatomie County et al. v. Lindsay Earls et al.*, 536 US 822, 2002.

The city of Tecumseh, Oklahoma, is a rural community located approximately 40 miles southeast of Oklahoma City. The School District administers all Tecumseh public schools. In the fall of 1998, the School District adopted the Student Activities Drug Testing Policy (Policy), which requires all middle and high school students to consent to drug testing in order to participate in any extracurricular activity. In practice, the Policy has been applied only to competitive extracurricular activities sanctioned by the Oklahoma Secondary Schools Activities Association, such as the Academic Team, Future Farmers of America, Future Homemakers of America, band, choir, pom pom, cheerleading, and athletics. Under the Policy, students are required to take a drug test before participating in an extracurricular activity, must submit to random drug testing while participating in that activity, and must agree to be tested at any time upon reasonable suspicion. The urinalysis tests are designed to detect only the use of illegal drugs, including amphetamines, marijuana, cocaine, opiates, and barbiturates, not medical conditions or the presence of authorized prescription medications. . . .

Determining Reasonableness

The Fourth Amendment to the United States Constitution protects "[t]he right of the people to be secure in their persons, houses, papers, and effects, against unreasonable searches and seizures." Searches by public school officials, such as the collection of urine samples, implicate Fourth Amendment interests. We must therefore review the School District's Policy for "reasonableness," which is the touchstone of the constitutionality of a governmental search.

In the criminal context, reasonableness usually requires a showing of probable cause. [We found in *Treasury Employees v. Von Raab*, that] the probable-cause standard, however, "is peculiarly related to criminal investigations" and may be unsuited to determining the reasonableness of administrative searches where the "Government seeks to *prevent* the development of hazardous conditions." The Court has also held that a warrant and finding of probable cause are unnecessary in the public school context because such requirements "would unduly interfere with the maintenance of the swift and informal disciplinary procedures [that are] needed."

Given that the School District's Policy is not in any way related to the conduct of criminal investigations, respondents do not contend that the School District requires probable cause before testing students for drug use. Respondents instead argue that drug testing must be based at least on some level of individualized suspicion. It is true that we generally determine the reasonableness of a search by balancing the nature of the intrusion on the individual's privacy against the promotion of legitimate governmental interests. But we have long held that "the Fourth Amendment imposes no irreducible requirement of [individualized] suspicion." [And in *United States v. Martinez Fuerte*, we wrote] "[I]n certain limited circumstances, the Government's need to discover such latent or hidden conditions, or to prevent their development, is sufficiently compelling to justify the intrusion on privacy entailed by conducting such searches without any measure of individualized suspicion." Therefore, [we ruled that] in the context of safety and administrative regulations, a search unsupported by probable cause may be reasonable "when 'special needs, beyond the normal need for law enforcement, make the warrant and probable-cause requirement impracticable.'"

"Special Needs"

Significantly, this Court has previously held that "special needs" inhere in the public school context. While schoolchildren do not shed their constitutional rights when they enter the schoolhouse, "Fourth Amendment rights . . . are different in public schools than elsewhere; the 'reasonableness' inquiry cannot disregard the schools' custodial and tutelary responsibility for children." In particular, a finding of individualized suspicion may not be necessary when a school conducts drug testing.

In *Vernonia*, this Court held that the suspicionless testing of athletes was constitutional. The Court, however, did not simply authorize all school drug testing, but rather conducted a fact-specific balancing of the intrusion on the children's Fourth Amendment rights against the promotion of legitimate governmental interests. Applying the principles of *Vernonia* to the somewhat different facts of this case, we conclude that Tecumseh's Policy is also constitutional.

The Nature of Privacy

We first consider the nature of the privacy interest allegedly compromised by the drug testing. As in *Vernonia*, the context of the public school environment serves as the backdrop for the analysis of the privacy interest at stake and the reasonableness of the drug testing policy in general.

A student's privacy interest is limited in a public school environment where the State is responsible for maintaining discipline, health, and safety. Schoolchildren are routinely required to submit to physical examinations and vaccinations against disease. Securing order in the school environment sometimes requires that students be subjected to greater controls than those appropriate for adults.

Respondents argue that because children participating in nonathletic extracurricular activities are not subject to regular physicals and communal undress, they have a stronger expectation of privacy than the athletes tested in *Vernonia*. This distinction, however, was not essential to our decision in *Vernonia*, which depended primarily upon the school's custodial responsibility and authority.

In any event, students who participate in competitive extracurricular activities voluntarily subject themselves to many of the same intrusions on their privacy as do athletes. Some of these clubs and activities require occasional off-campus travel and communal undress. All of them have their own rules and requirements for participating students that do not apply to the student body as a whole. For example, each of the competitive extracurricular activities governed by the Policy must abide by the rules of the Oklahoma Secondary Schools Activities Association, and a faculty sponsor monitors the students for compliance with the various rules dictated by the clubs and activities. This regulation of extracurricular activities further diminishes the expectation of privacy among schoolchildren. We therefore conclude that the students affected by this Policy have a limited expectation of privacy.

Next, we consider the character of the intrusion imposed

by the Policy. Urination is "an excretory function tradition-ally shielded by great privacy." But the "degree of intrusion" on one's privacy caused by collecting a urine sample "de-pends upon the manner in which production of the urine sample is monitored."

Under the Policy, a faculty monitor waits outside the closed restroom stall for the student to produce a sample and must "listen for the normal sounds of urination in order to guard against tampered specimens and to insure an accurate chain of custody." The monitor then pours the sample into two bottles that are sealed and placed into a mailing pouch along with a consent form signed by the student. This proce-dure is virtually identical to that reviewed in *Vernonia*, except that it additionally protects privacy by allowing male students to produce their samples behind a closed stall. Given that we considered the method of collection in *Vernonia* a "negligi-ble" intrusion, the method here is even less problematic. . . .

No Consequences

Moreover, the test results are not turned over to any law en-forcement authority. Nor do the test results here lead to the imposition of discipline or have any academic consequences. Rather, the only consequence of a failed drug test is to limit the student's privilege of participating in extracurricular activ-ities. Indeed, a student may test positive for drugs twice and still be allowed to participate in extracurricular activities. . . .

Given the minimally intrusive nature of the sample col-lection and the limited uses to which the test results are put, we conclude that the invasion of students' privacy is not sig-nificant.

Drug Abuse Is a Serious Concern

Finally, this Court must consider the nature and immediacy of the government's concerns and the efficacy of the Policy in meeting them. This Court has already articulated in detail the importance of the governmental concern in preventing drug use by schoolchildren. The drug abuse problem among our Nation's youth has hardly abated since *Vernonia* was de-cided in 1995. In fact, evidence suggests that it has only grown worse. As in *Vernonia*, "the necessity for the State to act is magnified by the fact that this evil is being visited not just upon individuals at large, but upon children for whom it has undertaken a special responsibility of care and direction." The health and safety risks identified in *Vernonia* apply with equal force to Tecumseh's children. Indeed, the nationwide drug epidemic makes the war against drugs a pressing concern in every school.

Additionally, the School District in this case has presented specific evidence of drug use at Tecumseh schools. Teachers testified that they had seen students who appeared to be under the influence of drugs and that they had heard students speaking openly about using drugs. A drug dog found marijuana cigarettes near the school parking lot. Police officers once found drugs or drug paraphernalia in a car driven by a Future Farmers of America member. And the school board president reported that people in the community were calling the board to discuss the "drug situation." We decline to second-guess the finding of the District Court that "[v]iewing the evidence as a whole, it cannot be reasonably disputed that the [School District] was faced with a 'drug problem' when it adopted the Policy."

Respondents consider the proffered evidence insufficient and argue that there is no "real and immediate interest" to justify a policy of drug testing nonathletes. We have recognized, however, that "[a] demonstrated problem of drug abuse . . . [is] not in all cases necessary to the validity of a testing regime," but that some showing does "shore up an assertion of special need for a suspicionless general search program." The School District has provided sufficient evidence to shore up the need for its drug testing program.

Testing Allowed on a Preventive Basis

Furthermore, this Court has not required a particularized or pervasive drug problem before allowing the government to conduct suspicionless drug testing. For instance, in *Von Raab* the Court upheld the drug testing of customs officials on a purely preventive basis, without any documented history of drug use by such officials. In response to the lack of evidence relating to drug use, the Court noted generally that "drug abuse is one of the most serious problems confronting our society today," and that programs to prevent and detect drug use among customs officials could not be deemed unreasonable. Likewise, the need to prevent and deter the substantial harm of childhood drug use provides the necessary immediacy for a school testing policy. Indeed, it would make little sense to require a school district to wait for a substantial portion of its students to begin using drugs before it was allowed to institute a drug testing program designed to deter drug use.

Given the nationwide epidemic of drug use, and the evidence of increased drug use in Tecumseh schools, it was entirely reasonable for the School District to enact this particular drug testing policy. . . .

An Effective Policy

We find that testing students who participate in extracurricular activities is a reasonably effective means of addressing the School District's legitimate concerns in preventing, deterring, and detecting drug use. While in *Vernonia* there might have been a closer fit between the testing of athletes and the trial court's finding that the drug problem was "fueled by the 'role model' effect of athletes' drug use," such a finding was not essential to the holding. *Vernonia* did not require the school to test the group of students most likely to use drugs, but rather considered the constitutionality of the program in the context of the public school's custodial responsibilities. Evaluating the Policy in this context, we conclude that the drug testing of Tecumseh students who participate in extracurricular activities effectively serves the School District's interest in protecting the safety and health of its students.

Within the limits of the Fourth Amendment, local school boards must assess the desirability of drug testing schoolchildren. In upholding the constitutionality of the Policy, we express no opinion as to its wisdom. Rather, we hold only that Tecumseh's Policy is a reasonable means of furthering the School District's important interest in preventing and deterring drug use among its schoolchildren.

"The lesson for U.S. students as they stand in line with urine bottles in hand is that the Fourth Amendment's guarantee [against unreasonable searches] is now a broken promise."

Testing Students for Drug Use Is Unreasonable

Richard Glen Boire

Richard Glen Boire argues in the following viewpoint that allowing schools to conduct random drug tests on students without a suspicion of wrongdoing treats students like crime suspects and forces them to prove their innocence. Drug tests for students who hope to participate in extracurricular activities do not deter students from taking drugs; studies show that most students who take part in extracurricular activities do not take drugs in the first place. Boire is the codirector and legal counsel for the Center for Cognitive Liberty and Ethics, a nonprofit legal and policy organization that works to promote freedom of thought.

As you read, consider the following questions:
1. What is Ruth Bader Ginsburg's opinion of testing students for drugs, as cited by Boire?
2. Why is a policy that bars students from extracurricular activities bad for society, according to the author?
3. What will happen to students who consider drug tests as normal as standardized tests, in the author's opinion?

Richard Glen Boire, "Dangerous Lessons," *Humanist*, vol. 62, November/December 2002, p. 39. Copyright © 2002 by Richard Glen Boire. Reproduced by permission.

The Supreme Court's ruling on June 27, 2002, giving public school authorities the green light to conduct random, suspicious drug testing of all junior and senior high school students wishing to participate in extracurricular activities, teaches by example. The lesson, unfortunately, is that the Fourth Amendment has become a historical artifact, a quaint relic from bygone days when our country honored the "scrupulous protection of constitutional freedoms of the individual," ([according to the Court in] *West Virginia State Board of Education v. Barnette*).

The Court's ruling turns logic on its head, giving the insides of students' bodies less protection than the insides of their backpacks, the contents of their bodily fluids less protection than the contents of their telephone calls. The decision elevates the myopic hysteria of a preposterous "zero-tolerance" drug war over basic values such as respect and dignity for our nation's young people.

Students Have Become Suspects

The Court's ruling treats America's teenage students like suspects. If a student seeks to participate in after-school activities, his or her urine can be taken and tested for any reason or for no reason at all. Gone are any requirements for individualized suspicion. Trust and respect have been replaced with a generalized distrust—an accusatory, authoritarian demand that students prove their "innocence" at the whim of the schoolmaster.

The Court majority reasoned that requiring students to yield up their urine for examination as a prerequisite to participating in extracurricular activities would serve as a deterrent to drug use. It reasoned that students who seek to join the debate team, write for the student newspaper, play in the marching band, or participate in any other after-school activities would be dissuaded from using drugs knowing that their urine would be tested.

While some students may indeed be deterred from using drugs, the conventional wisdom (supported by empirical data) is that students who participate in extracurricular activities are some of the least likely to use drugs. Noting this, Justice Ruth Bader Ginsburg, whose dissenting opinion was joined by Justices John Paul Stevens, Sandra Day O'Connor, and David Souter, harshly condemned random testing of such students and describes it as "unreasonable, capricious and even perverse." Even when applied to students who do use drugs, the Court's decision merely makes matters worse.

Students Continue to Experiment

The federal government has tried everything from threatening imprisonment to yanking student loans to spending hundreds of millions of dollars on "just say no" advertisements, and still some students continue to experiment with marijuana and other drugs. Like it or not, some students will use illegal drugs before graduating from high school, just as some students will have sex. Perhaps it's time to rethink the wisdom of declaring a "war on drugs" and adopt instead a realistic and effective strategy more akin to safe-sex education.

Ultimately, if a student does choose to experiment with an illegal drug (or a legal drug like alcohol), I suspect that many parents, like myself, would prefer that their child be taught the skills necessary to survive the experiment with as little harm as possible to self or others. The Drug Abuse Resistance Education (DARE) program—the nation's primary "drug education" curriculum—is taught by police officers, not drug experts, and is centered on intimidation and threats of criminal prosecution rather than on harm reduction. Random, suspicious urine testing fits the same tired mold.

The Ramifications of Drug Tests

Among the significant gaps in the majority's reasoning is its failure to consider the individual and social ramifications of deterring any student (whether or not they use drugs) from participating in after-school activities. Students who on principle prefer to keep their bodily fluids to themselves or who consider urine testing to be a gross invasion of privacy will be dissuaded from participating in after-school activities altogether. Similarly, students who do use drugs and who either test positive or forego the test for fear of what it might reveal will be banned from after-school activities and thus left to their own devices.

Extracurricular programs are valued for producing "well-rounded" students. Many adults look back on their extramural activities as some of the most educational, enriching, and formative experiences of their young lives. Extracurricular programs build citizenship, and for many universities participation in after-school clubs and academic teams is a decisive admissions criterion. Whether or not students use drugs, it makes no sense to bar them from the very activities that build citizenship and help prepare them for leadership roles in the workforce, or help them get into college. In other words, a policy that deters students or bans them outright from participating in extracurricular activities isn't just bad for students, it's bad for society.

Kelley. © 1989 by San Diego Union Copyright News Service. Reproduced by permission.

Aside from eviscerating the Fourth Amendment rights of the nation's twenty-three million public school students and imposing a punishment that harms society as much as it harms students, the decision foreshadows a constitutional dark age. When a young person is told to urinate in a cup within earshot of a school authority listening intently, and then ordered to turn over his or her urine for chemical examination, what "reasonable expectation of privacy" remains? When today's students graduate and walk out the schoolhouse gates, what will become of society's "reasonable expectation of privacy"?

Raised with the ever present specter of coercion and control where urine testing is as common as standardized testing, today's students will have little if any privacy expectations when they reach adulthood. As a result, what society presently regards as a "reasonable expectation of privacy" will be considerably watered down within a single generation. Rivers of urine will have eroded the Fourth Amendment—our nation's strictest restraint on the overreaching and strong-arm tendencies of some government police agents. Justice Ginsburg and the three other justices who joined her dissenting opinion aptly state "that [schools] are educating the young for citizenship is reason for scrupulous protection of Constitutional freedoms of the individual, if we are not to strangle the free mind at its source and teach youth to discount important principles of our government as mere platitudes."

The Greatest Tragedy

The U.S. government has just allocated another $19 billion to fight the so-called war on drugs, yet all we really have to show for it is a tattered Constitution and the largest prison population in the history of the world. Fellow U.S. citizens have been constructed as "the enemy" simply because they'd rather have a puff of marijuana than a shot of bourbon. And that is perhaps the greatest tragedy of the Court's ruling. The decision not only victimizes our children, but it makes them the enemy. Being a public school student is now synonymous with being a criminal suspect or a prisoner.

The values of trust and respect have been chased from the schoolyards and replaced with baseless suspicion and omnipresent policing. The lesson for U.S. students as they stand in line with urine bottles in hand is that the Fourth Amendment's guarantee is now a broken promise, yesterday's dusty trophy, and worthy only of lip service. The lesson for the rest of us is that the so-called war on drugs desperately needs rethinking.

> "It is rudimentary Fourth Amendment
> law that a search which has been consented
> to is not unreasonable."

Testing Pregnant Women for Drug Abuse Is Constitutional

Antonin Scalia, William Rehnquist, and Clarence Thomas

In the 1980s Charleston, South Carolina, hospitals began testing pregnant women for cocaine use in order to steer them into drug treatment programs. Later, the hospitals shared test results with the police with the aim of encouraging women to seek treatment in lieu of criminal sanctions. The following viewpoint is an excerpt of the dissenting opinion in *Ferguson v. City of Charleston*, a 2001 Supreme Court case in which the unconstitutionality of such drug tests was established. Justices Antonin Scalia, William Rehnquist, and Clarence Thomas argue that testing pregnant women for drug use, even without their knowledge or consent, and then giving the positive results to the police does not qualify as a "search," and therefore the practice is constitutional. They assert that the women gave their urine samples freely and willingly as part of a routine medical examination.

As you read, consider the following questions:
1. According to Scalia, what is the main objection of the women whose urine was tested for illegal drug use?
2. Which one act under review in the court case could conceivably be regarded as a search, in Scalia's opinion?
3. What was the "ultimate" goal of the police-cooperation policy, according to the authors?

Antonin Scalia, William Rehnquist, and Clarence Thomas, *Ferguson v. City of Charleston*, 532 US 67, March 21, 2001.

There is always an unappealing aspect to the use of doctors and nurses, ministers of mercy, to obtain incriminating evidence against the supposed objects of their ministration—although here, it is correctly pointed out, the doctors and nurses were ministering not just to the mothers but also to the children whom their cooperation with the police was meant to protect.[1] But whatever may be the correct social judgment concerning the desirability of what occurred here, that is not the issue in the present case. The Constitution does not resolve all difficult social questions, but leaves the vast majority of them to resolution by debate and the democratic process—which would produce a decision by the citizens of Charleston, through their elected representatives, to forbid or permit the police action at issue here. The question before us is a narrower one: whether, whatever the desirability of this police conduct, it violates the Fourth Amendment's prohibition of unreasonable searches and seizures. In my view, it plainly does not.

The Search at Issue

The first step in Fourth Amendment analysis is to identify the search or seizure at issue. What petitioners [the pregnant women whose urine was tested for drugs], the Court, and to a lesser extent the concurrence really object to is not the urine testing, but the hospital's reporting of positive drug-test results to police. But the latter is obviously not a search. At most it may be [as the U.S. Supreme Court wrote in *United States v. Calandra*] a "derivative use of the product of a past unlawful search," which, of course, "work[s] no new Fourth Amendment wrong" and "presents a question, not of rights, but of remedies." There is only one act that could conceivably be regarded as a search of petitioners in the present case: the *taking* of the urine sample. I suppose the *testing* of that urine for traces of unlawful drugs could be considered a search of sorts, but the Fourth Amendment protects only against searches of citizens' "persons, houses,

---

1. In Charleston, South Carolina, hospitals began to take urine samples from pregnant patients in order to steer cocaine users into treatment programs. Eventually, doctors and nurses shared test results with police, reasoning that the threat of criminal sanctions would encourage women to seek treatment.

papers, and effects"; and it is entirely unrealistic to regard urine as one of the "effects" (*i.e.*, part of the property) of the person who has passed and abandoned it. Some would argue, I suppose, that testing of the urine is prohibited by some generalized privacy right "emanating" from the "penumbras" of the Constitution (a question that is not before us); but it is not even arguable that the testing of urine that has been lawfully obtained is a Fourth Amendment search. (I may add that, even if it were, the factors legitimizing the taking of the sample, which I discuss below, would likewise legitimize the testing of it.)

The Samples Were Not Forcibly Obtained

It is rudimentary Fourth Amendment law that a search which has been consented to is not unreasonable. There is no contention in the present case that the urine samples were extracted forcibly. The only conceivable bases for saying that they were obtained without consent are the contentions (1) that the consent was coerced by the patients' need for medical treatment, (2) that the consent was uninformed because the patients were not told that the tests would include testing for drugs, and (3) that the consent was uninformed because the patients were not told that the results of the tests would be provided to the police.

Under our established Fourth Amendment law, the last two contentions would not suffice, even without reference to the special-needs doctrine. The Court's analogizing of this case to *Miranda* v. *Arizona*, and its claim that "standards of knowing waiver" apply, are flatly contradicted by our jurisprudence, which shows that using lawfully (but deceivingly) obtained material for purposes other than those represented, and giving that material or information derived from it to the police, is not unconstitutional. In *Hoffa* v. *United States*, "[t]he argument [was] that [the informant's] failure to disclose his role as a government informant vitiated the consent that the petitioner gave" for the agent's access to evidence of criminal wrongdoing. We rejected that argument, because "the Fourth Amendment [does not protect] a wrongdoer's misplaced belief that a person to whom he voluntarily confides his wrongdoing will not reveal it." Because the defendant had voluntarily provided access to the evidence, there was no reasonable expectation of privacy to invade. Abuse of trust is surely a sneaky and ungentlemanly thing, and perhaps there should be (as there are) laws against such conduct by the government. That, however, is immaterial for Fourth Amendment purposes, for "*however strongly* a defendant may trust an apparent colleague, his expectations in this respect are not protected by the Fourth Amendment when it turns out that the colleague is a government agent regularly communicating with the authorities." (Emphasis added.) The *Hoffa* line of cases, I may note, does not distinguish between operations meant to catch a criminal in the act, and those meant only to gather evidence of prior wrongdoing.

Confidential Relationships

Until today, we have *never* held—or even suggested—that material which a person voluntarily entrusts to someone else cannot be given by that person to the police, and used for whatever evidence it may contain. Without so much as discussing the point, the Court today opens a hole in our Fourth Amendment jurisprudence, the size and shape of which is entirely indeterminate. Today's holding would be remarkable enough if the confidential relationship violated by the police conduct were at least one protected by state law. It would be surprising to learn, for example, that in a State which recognizes a spousal evidentiary privilege the police cannot use evidence obtained from a cooperating husband or wife. But today's holding goes even beyond that, since there does not exist any physician-patient privilege in South Carolina. Since the Court declines even to discuss the issue, it leaves law enforcement officials entirely in the dark as to when they can use incriminating evidence obtained from "trusted" sources. Presumably the lines will be drawn in the case-by-case development of a whole new branch of Fourth Amendment jurisprudence, taking yet another social judgment (which confidential relationships ought not be invaded by the police) out of democratic control, and confiding it to the uncontrolled judgment of this Court—uncontrolled because there is no common-law precedent to guide it. I would adhere to our established law, which says that information obtained through violation of a relationship of trust is obtained consensually, and is hence not a search.

The Searches Were Reasonable

Maternal cocaine use is associated with a number of pregnancy complications, including low birth weight, premature labor, birth defects, and neurobehavioral problems. Even a single use of cocaine during pregnancy may result in separation of the placenta from the uterine wall—a condition that may threaten the life of the mother and the fetus—or a stroke in the fetus.

William W. Wilkins, *Ferguson v. City of Charleston*, July 13, 1999.

There remains to be considered the first possible basis for invalidating this search, which is that the patients were coerced to produce their urine samples by their necessitous circumstances, to wit, their need for medical treatment of their pregnancy. If that was coercion, it was not coercion applied by the government—and if such nongovernmental coercion sufficed, the police would never be permitted to use the ballistic evidence obtained from treatment of a patient with a bullet wound. And the Fourth Amendment would invalidate those many state laws that require physicians to report gunshot wounds, evidence of spousal abuse, and (like the South Carolina law relevant here,) evidence of child abuse.

Special Needs

I think it clear, therefore, that there is no basis for saying that obtaining of the urine sample was unconstitutional. The special-needs doctrine is thus quite irrelevant, since it operates only to validate searches and seizures that are otherwise unlawful. In the ensuing discussion, however, I shall assume (contrary to legal precedent) that the taking of the urine sample was (either because of the patients' necessitous circumstances, or because of failure to disclose that the urine would be tested for drugs, or because of failure to disclose that the results of the test would be given to the police) coerced. Indeed, I shall even assume (contrary to common sense) that the testing of the urine constituted an unconsented search of the patients' effects. On those assumptions, the special-needs doctrine *would* become relevant; and, properly applied, would validate what was done here.

The conclusion of the Court that the special-needs doctrine is inapplicable rests upon its contention that respondents "undert[ook] to obtain [drug] evidence from their patients" not for any medical purpose, but "*for the specific purpose of incriminating those patients.*" In other words, the purported medical rationale was merely a pretext; there was no special need. This contention contradicts the District Court's finding of fact that the goal of the testing policy "was not to arrest patients but to facilitate their treatment and protect both the mother and unborn child." This finding is binding upon us unless clearly erroneous. Not only do I find it supportable; I think any other finding would have to be overturned.

History of the Tests

The cocaine tests started in April 1989, *neither at police suggestion nor with police involvement.* Expectant mothers who tested positive were referred by hospital staff for substance-abuse treatment, an obvious health benefit to both mother and child. And, since "[i]nfants whose mothers abuse cocaine during pregnancy are born with a wide variety of physical and neurological abnormalities," which require medical attention, the tests were of additional medical benefit in predicting needed postnatal treatment for the child. Thus, in their origin—before the police were in any way involved—the tests had an immediate, not merely an "ultimate," purpose of improving maternal and infant health. Several months after the testing had been initiated, a nurse discovered that local police were arresting pregnant users of cocaine for child abuse, the hospitals general counsel wrote the county solicitor to ask "what, if anything, our Medical Center needs to do to assist you in this matter," (South Carolina law requires child abuse to be reported), the police suggested ways to avoid tainting evidence, and the hospital and police in conjunction used the testing program as a means of securing what the Court calls the "ultimate" health benefit of coercing drug-abusing mothers into drug treatment. Why would there be any reason to believe that, once this policy of using the drug tests for their "ultimate" health benefits had been adopted, use of them for their original, *immediate*, benefits somehow disappeared, and testing somehow became in its entirety nothing more than a "pretext" for obtaining grounds for arrest? On the face of it, this is incredible. The only evidence of the exclusively arrest-related purpose of the testing adduced by the Court is that the police-cooperation policy *itself* does not describe how to care for cocaine-exposed infants. But *of course* it does not, since that policy, adopted months after the cocaine testing was initiated, had as its only health object the "ultimate" goal of inducing drug treatment through threat of arrest. Does the Court really believe (or even *hope*) that, once invalidation of the program challenged here has been decreed, drug testing will cease?

In sum, there can be no basis for the Court's purported ability to "distinguis[h] this case from circumstances in which physicians or psychologists, in the course of ordinary medical procedures aimed at helping the patient herself, come across information that . . . is subject to reporting requirements," unless it is this: That the *addition* of a law-enforcement-related purpose *to* a legitimate medical purpose destroys applicability of the "special-needs" doctrine. But that is quite impossible, since the special-needs doctrine was developed, and is ordinarily employed, precisely to enable searches *by law enforcement officials* who, of course, ordinarily have a law enforcement objective. . . .

A Benign Purpose

As I indicated at the outset, it is not the function of this Court—at least not in Fourth Amendment cases—to weigh petitioners' privacy interest against the State's interest in meeting the crisis of "crack babies" that developed in the late 1980's. I cannot refrain from observing, however, that the outcome of a wise weighing of these interests is by no means clear. The initial goal of the doctors and nurses who conducted cocaine-testing in this case was to refer pregnant drug addicts to treatment centers, and to prepare for necessary treatment of their possibly affected children. When the doctors and nurses agreed to the program providing test results to the police, they did so because (in addition to the fact that child abuse was required by law to be reported) they wanted to use the sanction of arrest as a strong incentive for their addicted patients to undertake drug-addiction treatment. And the police themselves used it for that benign purpose, as is shown by the fact that only 30 of 253 women testing positive for cocaine were ever arrested, and only 2 of those prosecuted. It would not be unreasonable to conclude that today's judgment, authorizing the assessment of damages against the county solicitor and individual doctors and nurses who participated in the program, proves once again that no good deed goes unpunished.

But as far as the Fourth Amendment is concerned: There was no unconsented search in this case. And if there was, it would have been validated by the special-needs doctrine. For these reasons, I respectfully dissent.

"The singling out of drugs, particularly crack cocaine, from all the other ways in which the fetus can be harmed demonstrates the discriminatory impact and purpose of these laws."

Testing Pregnant Women for Drug Abuse Is Discriminatory

Lawrence O. Gostin

In the following viewpoint Lawrence O. Gostin discusses a 2001 Supreme Court case in which pregnant women sued a hospital that tested them—without their knowledge or consent—for cocaine use and then turned positive results over to the police. The Supreme Court ruled that the drug tests were an invasion of the women's privacy. Gostin contends that the policy could have resulted in women avoiding prenatal care in an attempt to avoid incarceration for drug use. Furthermore, he asserts, the drug tests were discriminatory because the majority of women who were tested were low-income minorities. Gostin is a law professor at Georgetown University Law School in Washington, D.C., and a professor of law and public health at Johns Hopkins University.

As you read, consider the following questions:

1. What are some of the offenses women have been charged with to punish them for behavior that endangers their fetuses, as cited by the author?
2. In what ways did the Supreme Court distinguish the Ferguson case from other drug-testing cases, according to Gostin?

During the last two decades, states have sought to punish pregnant women for behavior that endangers their fetuses, often without success. Prosecutors have used various novel legal theories, including child abuse and neglect, delivery and distribution of controlled substances, and involuntary manslaughter. Some states have enacted special laws criminalizing prenatal drug use. Other states have authorized "any necessary measures" to protect the fetus. These measures include civil commitment for pregnant women who use drugs and cash incentives for crack-using women to become sterilized.

Ferguson v. City of Charleston

During the height of concern for fetal rights, in the late 1980s, the Medical University of South Carolina (MUSC) devised a policy, in cooperation with law enforcement officials, for screening pregnant patients for cocaine use. Women who tested positive would be turned over to police and threatened with prosecution to provide "the necessary leverage" to force them into treatment. The policy specified criteria for determining which pregnant women should be tested (targeting, for example, women who had obtained no prenatal care or late or incomplete prenatal care, and women known to have previously abused drugs or alcohol abuse). It also required urine samples to be handled through an appropriate "chain of custody" to ensure that they could be used as evidence in a criminal trial; and it detailed the offenses with which the woman could be charged, depending on the age of the fetus. The charges included simple possession, possession and distribution to a minor, and child neglect. The policy made no mention of any change in the woman's prenatal care and did not prescribe any special treatment for newborns. More than forty women were arrested under the MUSC program, and some who tested positive for cocaine during labor were taken to jail in handcuffs or leg shackles shortly after giving birth. Under South Carolina law, a viable fetus historically has been regarded as a person; on this basis, the state's Supreme Court has held that the ingestion of cocaine during the third trimester of pregnancy constitutes criminal child neglect.

In 1999, the U.S. Court of Appeals for the Fourth Circuit (well-known for its conservative judicial activism), held that regardless of whether the women provided informed consent, the MUSC testing program was justified by the "special need" of stopping drug use by pregnant women. [In 2001] in *Ferguson v. City of Charleston*, the Supreme Court overturned the Fourth Circuit, holding that a public hospital's policy of subjecting pregnant women to nonconsensual drug tests without a warrant, and turning positive test results over to police, violates the Fourth Amendment's proscription against unreasonable searches.

Special Needs

Although the Fourth Amendment is popularly perceived as applying solely to personal or residential searches, the Supreme Court has long recognized that the collection and subsequent analysis of biological samples is a "search." In most criminal cases, a search is unreasonable unless it is accomplished pursuant to a judicial warrant issued upon probable cause, and if a warrant is impracticable, then the courts require, minimally, "reasonable suspicion" based on an individualized assessment. The Supreme Court has held, however, that when the state has "special needs beyond the normal need for law enforcement," the warrant and probable or reasonable cause requirements may not be applicable. In three drug testing cases, the Court applied the special needs exception to sustain drug tests for railway employees involved in train accidents, Customs Service employees seeking promotion to certain sensitive positions, and high school students participating in interscholastic sports. In a fourth case, the Court struck down drug testing for candidates for certain state offices.

The Supreme Court in *Ferguson* held that the MUSC screening program did not fit within the "closely guarded category of constitutionally permissible suspicionless searches." The Court distinguished *Ferguson* from its previous cases because MUSC conducted drug tests and turned the results over to police without the patients' knowledge or consent. The invasion of privacy was far more substantial because of the physician-patient relationship. A patient has a "reasonable expectation of privacy . . . that the results of [diagnostic] tests will not be shared with nonmedical personnel without her consent." The Court stressed that the law enforcement purpose in *Ferguson* was critically important. The "central and indispensable feature of the policy from its inception was the use of law enforcement to coerce the patients into substance abuse treatment." Even though the ultimate purpose was beneficent, the purpose it actually serves "is ultimately indistinguishable from the general interest in crime control."

SHARPNACK
©1997

URINALYSIS

Sharpnack. © 1997 by Joe Sharpnack. Reproduced by permission.

Ferguson is an important judicial precedent not only because it recognizes the special importance of the therapeutic relationship and safeguards patient privacy, but also because it limits the application to the special needs exception in cases involving medical screening. Most courts have assumed a permissive posture when reviewing government screening programs. Government has been permitted to require HIV testing of firefighters, military personnel, immigrants, and sex offenders, for example. The Supreme Court's decision in *Ferguson* may make courts more willing to scrutinize compulsory public health screening programs.

Gender, Race, and Class

Policies that coerce or punish pregnant women purport to protect the public's health. On closer reflection, however, they may be harmful and reflect subtle forms of discrimination. Conscripting health care professionals to perform law enforcement undermines patient trust, which may lead to a reduction in prenatal care and even in the overall use of health services. Further, policies or laws that coerce or punish pregnant women may encourage more abortions; a woman who must choose between abortion and incarceration may prefer the former.

These policies raise questions of fairness because they are applied exclusively to women and predominantly to poor women of color. Men who endanger the health of the fetus through spousal abuse, for example, are not subjected to special penalties related to fetal protection. Further, even though these policies are neutral on their face, they are applied disproportionately to the poorest, most vulnerable members of society. Illicit drug laws of all kinds are applied more often to racial minorities and the poor; and crack cocaine laws exacerbate that effect. The singling out of drugs, particularly crack cocaine, from all the other ways in which the fetus can be harmed demonstrates the discriminatory impact and purpose of these laws. Consider the most recent data suggesting that the effects of crack on fetal health have been significantly exaggerated due to the confounding effects of an impoverished environment and the physical and sexual abuse experienced by many poor, minority women. Compare the effects on fetuses caused by cocaine with those caused by tobacco or alcoholic beverages, and consider the absence of government coercion in these areas. Predominately poor people of color are punished for risks to their fetuses that are considerably less than the risks accepted by more wealthy mainstream populations.

The Charleston policy illustrates the discriminatory effects. The criteria used to determine who would be subjected to testing included indicia that are prevalent within low-income and minority populations, such as the absence of prenatal care and a previous documented history of substance abuse. The policy was implemented in only one hospital in the state—the public hospital located in a poor community. Many indigent women who were not using illicit drugs were tested without their knowledge or consent. Of the forty-one arrests made pursuant to the Charleston policy, forty were of black women. Physicians who found substances often associated with middle and upper class populations, such as methamphetamine and heroin, made referrals to social services, not to law enforcement.

One highly unusual aspect of *Ferguson* was that all of the friend of the court briefs opposed the MUSC policy, including an amicus brief filed by the Rutherford Institute, a staunch pro-life organization. Yet Justice [Antonin] Scalia, joined by [William] Rehnquist and [Clarence] Thomas, dissented: the fact that the public officials who participated in the program might now face damages for violating the women's constitutional rights "proves once again that no good deed goes unpunished." The dissent argued that health care professionals were "ministering not just to the mothers but also to the children whom their cooperation with the police was meant to protect."

Justice Scalia is not wrong when he suggests that sound public health policies should protect the health and well-being of the fetus as well as the mother. A great deal more can be done to safeguard maternal and child health, including providing universal access to high quality pre- and postnatal maternal care, mental health care, drug and alcohol treatment, health education, and healthy living environments in early childhood. Offering pregnant women medical, social, and educational services does not erect a false dichotomy between the interests of mother and child, but sees their interests as intertwined. Such policies are effective, fair, and protective of constitutional rights to bodily integrity and medical privacy.

"It IS the employer's business *when drug abuse OFF the job will affect performance or safety ON the job."*

Workplace Testing Reduces Drug Use

OHS Health and Safety Services, Inc.

OHS Health and Safety Services, Inc. administers drug- and alcohol-testing programs in the workplace. In the following viewpoint the company argues that the use of illegal drugs is a problem for small and large businesses. Drug abuse affects workers' productivity and attendance, and is also responsible for an increase in accidents both on and off the job. In addition, drug users also sell drugs at the workplace and steal from their employers and coworkers in order to support their habit. OHS asserts that drug-testing programs are an effective way to combat this problem; few drug users are willing to apply for jobs at companies that test their employees for drug use, and many drug users stop abusing drugs for fear of being caught.

As you read, consider the following questions:

1. What percentage of adult Americans who use illegal drugs are employed, as cited by the author?
2. What are three misconceptions about "false positives" on drug tests, according to OHS?
3. In the author's opinion, why is it an employer's business what an employee does when not at work?

1) *How big is America's drug problem?* *BIG!* The U.S. Government reports that, in the last month, 9.7 million Americans used marijuana and 1.9 million used cocaine! Due to "hybrid" planting and illicit "lab" techniques, marijuana and other drugs today are stronger, cheaper, and far more lethal than ever.

Drug Abuse Costs Businesses

2) But, is it really a problem for small business owners as well as for Corporate America? Yes! More than seven out of ten (77%) of Americans 18+ who engage in illicit drug use are *employed.* That's 9.4 MILLION *employees* doing drugs! (How many work for YOUR company?)

As a result, the vast majority of businesses—small and large—suffer from substantial decreased productivity and increased accidents (accidents both on and off the job—the latter, of course, affecting attendance, and work performance while ON the job). Drug abuse also dramatically increases medical claims and workers' compensation payouts. These more frequent claims, in turn, directly cause increases in the premiums paid by the employer for medical and workers' comp coverage. (In fact, in the case of "medical" premiums, even employees end up paying higher contributions out of their paycheck every month!)

Additionally, employee drug abuse definitely leads to the abusers' increased absenteeism and taking more than the average number of "sick days"—time off often paid for by their employer. While abusers are "buzzed" on the job, they are responsible for more product defects, missed deadlines, incomplete projects, or inaccurate work. To support their drug habit, abusers are responsible for higher than normal instances of employee *theft*—not just from their company, but from their fellow employees, too. They also can be counted on for more employee equipment *loss*, employee equipment *damage*, and other problems—including *drug-dealing* (again, to support their own drug habit)!

Roger Smith, the former chairman of General Motors, said drug abuse costs GM $1 billion a year.

3) What are employers doing about the drug problem? Hundreds of thousands of employers—small and large—are now adopting and implementing one or more of the following: company-wide anti-drug abuse policies; comprehensive drug-abuse education and drug awareness programs; drug testing programs; and employee assistance and rehabilitation (EAP) programs. More than fifty (>50) million drug tests were performed in the U.S. [in 1999].

Drug Testing Is Accurate

4) Is drug testing accurate? Yes, when done properly. The typical procedure is a two-step process in which a urine sample (specimen) is divided in half, and the first half is tested using a relatively simple, inexpensive, yet highly accurate test (usually an "immunoassay"). If the result of that initial test is "negative" the lab will report the test as "negative" and no additional testing will be performed on that specimen. On the other hand, if the result of the first test is "positive", then a second test is conducted on the second half of the original sample using a different testing process that serves to "confirm" whether or not the first analysis was accurate.

This second ("confirmatory") test is performed using a more sophisticated and more expansive technique such as gas chromatography/mass spectrometry (GC/MS) or thin-layer chromatography (TLC). Only if *both* halves of a specimen show up "positive" by these two separate testing methods (and using portions of the same urine) is it then reported as a "positive" by the lab. The first test (by immunoassay) is 97–99% accurate, while the second test (by GC/MS or TLC) is virtually 100.00% accurate from a scientific standpoint. Because of this Industry-standard, two-step, "fail-safe" process, the lab's report of the specimen as "positive" (AFTER a second, confirmatory test) will—virtually 100% of the time—be upheld in a Court of Law if the person who was tested should choose to try and legally "challenge" that result.

5) But can't you "beat" a drug test? Yes, you "can", but the odds against it are very long and getting longer all the time. The opportunity for adulteration or substitution generally is limited by the integrity of the collection and testing process, and at any rate is detectable in most cases at the laboratory. The increasing popularity of "on site" specimen collection, too, has greatly contributed to the reduction of specimen

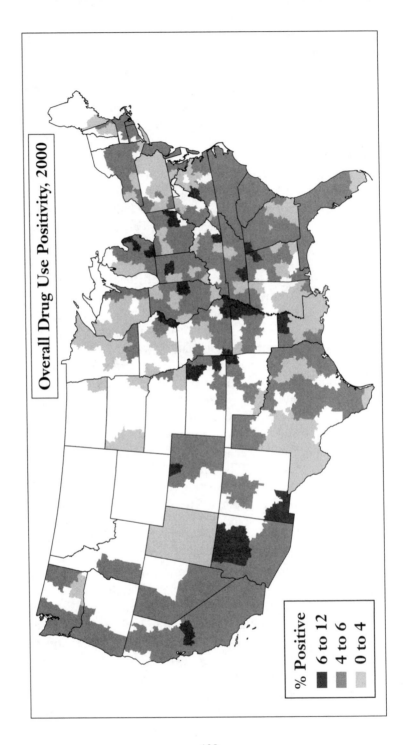

Overall Drug Use Positivity, 2000

% Positive
■ 6 to 12
■ 4 to 6
■ 0 to 4

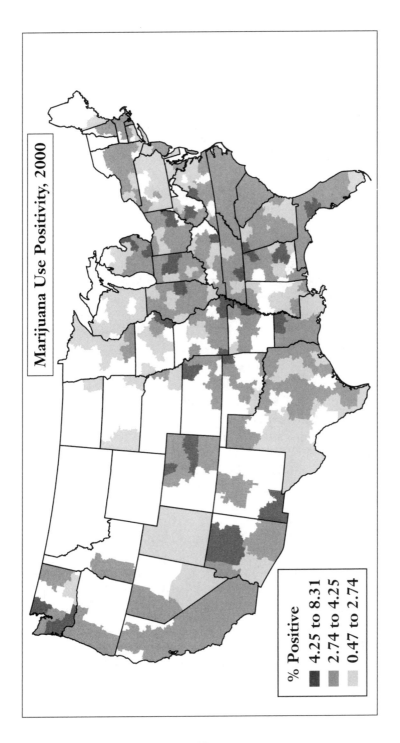

Marijuana Use Positivity, 2000

% Positive
■ 4.25 to 8.31
■ 2.74 to 4.25
░ 0.47 to 2.74

adulteration or substitution by donors attempting to cheat the system.

False Positives

6) What about "false positives"? Most of the popular stories about "things" that falsely trigger a "positive" drug-test result are based on misconceptions. These "things" normally either:

• Don't show up at all (e.g., "second-hand" marijuana smoke does NOT trigger a positive)

• Are not detected at a sufficient level to produce a false positive (e.g., a normal amount of ingested poppy seeds will NOT trigger a positive for "opiates")

• Are easily distinguishable as "false" in the laboratory

Some activities, such as a non-pot-smoker being sealed in a phone booth with four marijuana smokers who smoke pot non-stop for eight hours, "might" trigger a false positive, but for most people this scenario does not even come close to being a valid concern. What *does* occasionally happen to cause a positive, though, is *properly used prescription medicines* or some other *legitimate* justification for testing "positive" on a drug test. This is where the Medical Review Officer (MRO) becomes invaluable in the process of "confirming" lab positives.

The MRO speaks directly with the employee involved. The MRO gives the employee a chance to prove (e.g., by presenting a prescription) that the drugs found in their system were legitimately prescribed. In such cases where proof is presented, then, the employee (although found "positive" by the lab test) will—instead—be officially (and *correctly*) reported to their employer by the MRO as "negative".

7) Is drug testing legal? There are some restrictions on drug testing in a few states. But, generally, employers have a right to establish a written drug test company policy that requires that employees be drug free *and* to implement drug testing as part of their program. In any case, federal [Department of Transportation] (DOT) regulations take precedence over any local and state restrictions in the case of DOT-regulated companies.

8) How common is drug testing? In 1983, only 3% of the Fortune 200 companies were testing one or more classes of job applicants or employees. By 1991, that number had climbed to 97%.

No Right to Illegal Behavior

9) But is it any business of an employer's "what" an employee does in the privacy of his or her own home on a Saturday night? First of all, there is no Constitutional or other legally protected right to engage in *illegal* conduct in the privacy of one's own home or anyone else's. In any case, employee drug testing is *not* done in the employee's home! Employee testing is always done while the employee is *"on* the job", *about* to start work, or *immediately after* their shift.

Regardless, it IS the employer's *business* when drug abuse OFF the job will affect performance or safety ON the job. Drug use that can adversely affect job attendance or performance can and should be the concern of the employee's employer. The employer should have a right to be concerned about an employee's substance abuse "at home", or "the night before" if it may adversely impact on his business production and on his and other's workplace safety "the next day". (U.S. employers have *legal obligation* to provide each and every one of their employees with "a healthy and safe workplace environment"—it's the LAW!)

Employee drug-use was documented in a study which found that, of those employees seeking help on a "cocaine hotline":

- 64% admitted that drugs had adversely affected their job performance
- 44% said they had *sold* drugs to other employees
- 18% said they had *stolen* from co-workers to support their habits

(Why should ANY employer have to put up with this at a business that THEY OWN?)

Another study by the U.S. government found that those who illicitly used drugs are:

- 3.6 times more likely to injure themselves or *another person* in the workplace accident
- 5 times more likely to be injured in an accident *off the job* which, in turn, affects their attendance and/or performance *on the job*
- 5 times more likely to file a Workers' Compensation claim
- One-third less productive than non-drug using employees
- Incur 300% higher medical costs than non-drug using employees

(Again, we ask—Why should ANY employer have to put up with this?)

10) But don't many people use drugs without *losing control?* Some start that way, but drug-use tends to escalate with time. Using "a little" turns into using "a lot". Also, there is often a "gateway" effect: the initial use of what many perceive as less serious drugs (e.g., marijuana) can lead to the use of more serious drugs (e.g., cocaine); sporadic use can develop into chronic use; and people who never considered addiction a possibility for themselves personally can become desperate addicts. Further, the psychology of addiction is such that it includes a process of denial; *addicts very seldom admit their addiction voluntarily.*

Furthermore, even a "casual" user can present a substantial safety and health risk on the job to themselves, to their co-workers, and to the company's customers.

Crime on the Job

11) What about drug or alcohol-related crime on the job? Drug abuse has a major impact on workplace crime. Employees who have a $1,000–$3,000 a month narcotic habit do not usually support that habit with "just" their paycheck. General Motors, for example, has arrested over 500 employees for *dealing* drugs on the job! Crime in the forms of stealing from co-workers, blackmail, ties to organized crime, and the violence associated with drug dealing all threaten a health and safety workplace environment wherever drug abusers are employed. Further, the workplace often provides the perfect cover for *buying* and *selling* drugs.

In fact, drug-abuse treatment professionals state that a drug abuser's "JOB" is usually the one thing abusers will do ANYTHING to *hold on to*, for several reasons:

Denial—employees convince themselves that people who "work" (like themselves) are not addicted

Money—employees need a consistent paycheck to help support their drug habits

Opportunity—employees are provided with, both chances to steal (from their employer *and* from fellow employees) and also to *deal* drugs that they would not have if they were *unemployed*

IT'S A "GIVEN": If you have drug *users* in your company, you probably have drug *dealers* in your company!

12) *[How long do drugs stay in your system?]* In very large part, it will vary depending on a person's physiological makeup (e.g., height, weight, age, current state of health, state of mind). Other considerations include the person's "frequency" (1× per day? 3–5× per day?) and "quantity" of use and the "length of time" (days? weeks? months?) of their drug-use prior to testing. However, for most people, detectable levels of the following drugs stay in the body for these periods of time:

- Marijuana, 2–5 days (the daily, heavy user can sometimes be detected up to 30+ days)
- Cocaine, 1–2 days
- Amphetamines, 1–2 days
- Opiates, 1–3 days
- Phencyclidine (PCP), 1–8 days
- Alcohol, less than 24 hours

For *chronic* users, drugs (other than alcohol) can be retained in the system much longer after their last use—up to 60 days in extreme situations.

Marijuana Is Dangerous

13) *OK, so* cocaine *is serious, but just how dangerous can* marijuana *really be?* Marijuana can be a highly addictive drug. It is retained in the fatty tissue of the body for several days and it can cause impairment long after the "high" wears off. A study was conducted at Stanford University in which airline pilots smoked relatively weak government-issued marijuana cigarettes for the test. Each pilot was then tested on computerized flight simulators. The testing resulted in simulated airline "crashes" right after the marijuana use. More alarming, however, was the fact that it also resulted in "crashes" FULLY 24 HOURS LATER, *when every pilot reported "no residual effects" and each had stated they had "no reservations" about flying!* Also, an incident at American Airlines showed the dangers of marijuana in the workplace. One computer operator who was high on marijuana while working at the airline's central reservations system failed to load a tape in the computer at a critical juncture. The result was 8 hours of down time for the entire reservations system, significant data erasures, and a $19 million loss for the airline.

14) What specimens are commonly used for drug testing? Urine specimen analysis is the most common by far. Blood analysis is not common because it's "invasive" (needle used). "Oral" fluids analysis has recently become available, however it does *not* do as good a job detecting marijuana-use as is provided by testing urine. Hair specimen analysis is gaining in use. It will detect drug-use as far back as ninety (90) days, much longer than it is detectable in the urine. Random hair testing is the method of choice for the majority of Nevada casinos.

15) What about employee alcohol *abuse?* Alcohol remains the number one drug of abuse in America. It hurts more employees and their families than all other drugs combined. Furthermore, particularly among younger workers, poly-drug abuse (involving alcohol and other drugs) is increasingly common.

Rights at Stake

16) Aren't there important individual rights at stake? Yes, very important. That is precisely why employers should make every reasonable effort to minimize the intrusiveness of their drug abuse prevention programs to their workers. Employees have the rights to *privacy, confidentiality, accuracy* in testing if the company tests for drugs, and a written drug testing policy that is fairly and consistently enforced.

In order to guarantee these rights, employers should take the following steps:

Develop a written drug testing policy for the employees that is well thought-out and communicated

- Even-handed enforcement per that policy
- Preservation of an employee's privacy—making sure that only those with a "need to know" will know about a violation of the company's written policy
- In testing programs, use of confirmation tests, the maintaining of chain-of-custody, use of accredited laboratories and a certified MRO, and, fair application to the work force at large.

Moreover, public safety, efficient performance, product integrity, and employee morale are also legitimate interests which must be served. There is also too little said about the rights of employees who do NOT abuse drugs. Non-users have an absolute *right* to work in a *safe* working environment and to NOT have *their* jobs and benefits undermined by drug abusers!

Employees Support Drug Testing

17) What are employees' views about workplace drug testing? A recent national Gallup survey of employees demonstrated an increasing *intolerance* among employees for drug abuse and drug abusers, and an *acceptance* of employers taking strong steps to provide drug-free workplaces. The respondents said:

• 28% of employees who were asked what they thought was the greatest problem facing the United States today answered "drugs". That response was given more than two-and-a-half times more frequently than the second most common answer.

• 22% of employees whose companies have drug testing programs feel it is "not strong enough", while only 2% think it is "too strong".

• 97+% of employees favor drug testing in the workplace at least under some circumstances.

18) But, come on now . . . does workplace drug abuse really affect me? Drug abuse affects all citizens in the form of higher taxes, higher insurance rates, more crime, higher health care costs, and higher consumer prices. It also affects most of us as employees. A major telecommunications company reports that 40% of its health care costs are attributable to substance abuse!

19) Do company drug-abuse prevention programs work? First of all, *drug testing* works. As a result of advertised, high-profile drug-abuse prevention programs enacted at many companies, many drug users don't even apply there (at companies that do drug testing). Some of those who do apply will then stop using for fear of being caught, and some who are later "caught" will often undergo treatment and go straight.

There are numerous success stories in both the private and public sectors, but perhaps none as dramatic as the U.S. Navy's: a decrease since the 1980's to under 4% (down from 28%) of its active personnel engaged in illicit drug use (i.e., found positive when tested). This is specifically due to Navy's implementation back in the 80's of a comprehensive drug abuse prevention program—including monthly *random* drug testing of all *active* and *reserve* duty personnel—that continues even today.

6

"Drug testing became broadly accepted without any firm evidence that it does what it's supposed to do: improve safety, reduce costs, and boost productivity."

Workplace Testing Has Not Been Proven to Reduce Drug Use

Jacob Sullum

The federal government has strong-armed large American corporations into testing their employees for illegal drug use, asserts Jacob Sullum in the following viewpoint, by requiring government contractors to maintain a "drug-free workplace." Other companies have begun testing applicants and employees for illegal drug use because they are afraid of attracting drug users if they do not test and their competitors do. However, Sullum contends that there is little evidence confirming that drug testing is effective at improving productivity, work performance, and reducing drug use. In addition, employers rarely test applicants or employees for alcohol abuse, which is a far bigger drug problem affecting the workplace. Sullum is a syndicated columnist.

As you read, consider the following questions:

1. What was the surest way businesses could demonstrate compliance with the Drug-Free Workplace Act of 1988, in Sullum's opinion?
2. Approximately how many drug tests are performed each year in the United States, as cited by the author?
3. What percentage of the population meets the criteria for "any substance use disorder," as reported by Sullum?

Jacob Sullum, "Urine—Or You're Out," *Reason*, vol. 34, November 2002, p. 37. Copyright © 2002 by the Reason Foundation, 3415 S. Sepulveda Blvd., Suite 400, Los Angeles, CA 90034, www.reason.com. Reproduced with permission.

Federal policies requiring or encouraging drug testing by private employers include transportation regulations, conditions attached to government contracts, and propaganda aimed at convincing companies that good corporate citizens need to take an interest in their workers' urine. From the government's perspective, it does not matter whether this urological fixation is good for a company's bottom line. And given the meagerness of the evidence that drug testing makes economic sense, it probably would be much less popular with employers if it were purely a business practice rather than a weapon of prohibition. If it weren't for the war on drugs, it seems likely that employers would treat marijuana and other currently illegal intoxicants the way they treat alcohol, which they view as a problem only when it interferes with work.

Why Test?

Civilian drug testing got a big boost in 1986, when President [Ronald] Reagan issued an executive order declaring that "drugs will not be tolerated in the Federal workplace." The order asserted that "the use of illegal drugs, on or off duty," undermines productivity, health, safety, public confidence, and national security. In addition to drug testing based on "reasonable suspicion" and following accidents, Reagan authorized testing applicants for government jobs and federal employees in "sensitive positions." Significantly, the order was based on the premise that "the Federal government, as the largest employer in the Nation, can and should show the way towards achieving drug-free workplaces." Two years later, Congress approved the Drug-Free Workplace Act of 1988, which demanded that all federal grant recipients and many contractors "maintain a drug-free workplace." Although the law did not explicitly require drug testing, in practice this was the surest way to demonstrate compliance.

Private employers, especially big companies with high profiles and lucrative government contracts (or hopes of getting them), soon followed the government's lead. In its surveys of large employers, the American Management Association found that the share with drug testing programs increased from 21 percent in 1987 to 81 percent in 1996. A 1988 survey by the Bureau of Labor Statistics estimated that drug testing was required by 16 percent of work sites nationwide. Four years later, according to a survey by the statistician Tyler Hartwell and his colleagues, the share had increased to nearly half. In the 1997 National Household Survey on Drug Abuse (the source of the most recent nationwide data), 49 percent of respondents said their employers required some kind of drug testing.

As many as 50 million drug tests are performed each year in this country, generating revenue in the neighborhood of $1.5 billion. That's in addition to the money earned by specialists, such as consultants and medical review officers, who provide related services. Drug testing mainly affects pot smokers, because marijuana is much more popular than other illegal drugs and has the longest detection window. Traces of marijuana can be detected in urine for three or more days after a single dose, so someone who smoked a joint on Friday night could test positive on Monday morning. Daily marijuana smokers can test positive for weeks after their last puff. Because traces linger long after the drug's effects have worn off, a positive result does not indicate intoxication or impairment.

No Clear Evidence

The relevance of such test results to job performance is by no means clear. But in the late 1980s and early '90s, government propaganda and alarmist press coverage combined to persuade employers that they could no longer rely on traditional methods for distinguishing between good and bad workers. "When employers read in *Time* and *Newsweek* and *U.S. News & World Report* that there was an epidemic of drug abuse in America, they got scared like everyone else," says Lewis Maltby, president of the National Workrights Institute and a leading critic of drug testing. "They didn't want some pothead in their company causing a catastrophe and killing someone. Drug testing was the only answer that anyone presented to them, so they took it." Because drug testing was seen as an emergency measure, its costs and benefits were never carefully evaluated. "Most firms are understandably rigorous about making major investment decisions," Maltby says, "but drug testing was treated as an exception."

My interviews with officials of companies that do drug testing—all members of the Institute for a Drug-Free Workplace—tended to confirm this assessment. They all seemed to feel that drug testing was worthwhile, but they offered little evidence to back up that impression.

Link Staffing Services, a Houston-based temp agency, has been testing applicants since the late 1980s. "In the industry that we are in," says Amy Maxwell, Link's marketing manager, "a lot of times we get people with undesirable traits, and drug testing can screen them out real quick." In addition to conducting interviews and looking at references, the company does background checks, gives applicants a variety of aptitude tests, and administers the Link Occupational Pre-employment Evaluation, a screening program that "helps identify an applicant's tendency towards characteristics such as absenteeism, theft and dishonesty, low productivity, poor attitude, hostility, and drug use or violence." Although the drug testing requirement may help impress Link's customers, it seems unlikely that urinalysis adds something useful to the information from these other screening tools. Asked if drug testing has affected accident rates or some other performance indicator, Maxwell says, "We probably don't track that, because we have other things that [applicants] have to pass."

Employees Are Not Tested

Eastman Kodak, which makes photographic supplies and equipment, tests all applicants in the U.S. but tests employees (except for those covered by Department of Transportation regulations) only when there's cause for suspicion of drug-related impairment. Wayne Lednar, Eastman Kodak's corporate medical director, says safety was the company's main concern when it started doing drug testing in the 1980s. "Our safety performance has substantially improved in the last 10 years on a worldwide basis, not just in the United States," Lednar says. "That improvement, however, is not one [for which] the drug testing approach in the U.S. can be the major explanation. A very large worldwide corporation initiative driven by line management is really what I think has made the difference in terms of our safety performance."

David Spratt, vice president for medical services at Crown

Cork & Seal, a Philadelphia-based packaging manufacturer, says that when the company started doing drug testing in the early 1990s, "there was a concern that employees who used drugs were more likely to have problems in the workplace, be either the perpetrators or the victims of more accidents or more likely to be less productive." But like Eastman Kodak, Crown Cork & Seal does not randomly test employees; once they're hired, workers can use drugs without getting into trouble, as long as they do their jobs well. "What drives our concern is work performance," Spratt says. "If there is such a thing [as] 'recreational use,' we would probably not find that out."

Asked if the company has any evidence that drug testing has been effective, Spratt says: "That's not typically the way these things start out. They typically start out with, 'We gotta do drug testing, because the guy up the street is doing drug testing, and the people who walk in and see his sign will come down and sign up with us for a job.' We're going to get the skewed. . . .They will be a different group who may be less than desirable."

Margot Brown, senior director of communications and public affairs at Motorola, which makes semiconductors, cell phones, and two-way radios, says that when the company started doing drug testing in 1983, "They were trying to control the quality of their products and the safety of their work force." Asked whether the goals were accomplished, she says: "Our productivity per employee did go up substantially. . . .Who knows if that was coincidental or not? Those were good years for Motorola."

Weak Studies

As those remarks suggest, drug testing became broadly accepted without any firm evidence that it does what it's supposed to do: improve safety, reduce costs, and boost productivity. "Despite beliefs to the contrary," concluded a comprehensive 1994 review of the scientific literature by the National Academy of Sciences, "the preventive effects of drug-testing programs have never been adequately demonstrated." While allowing for the possibility that drug testing could make sense for a particular employer, the academy's panel of experts cautioned that little was known about the impact of drug use on work performance. "The data obtained in worker population studies," it said, "do not provide clear evidence of the deleterious effects of drugs other than alcohol on safety and other job performance indicators."

Drug Tests Are Unreliable

The drug screens used by most companies are not reliable. These tests yield false positive results at least 10 percent, and possibly as much as 30 percent, of the time. Experts concede that the tests are unreliable. At a recent conference, 120 forensic scientists, including some who worked for manufacturers of drug tests, were asked, "Is there anybody who would submit urine for drug testing if his career, reputation, freedom or livelihood depended on it?" Not a single hand was raised.

Although more accurate tests are available, they are expensive and infrequently used. And even the more accurate tests can yield inaccurate results due to laboratory error. A survey by the National Institute on Drug Abuse, a government agency, found that 20 percent of the labs surveyed mistakenly reported the presence of illegal drugs in drug-free urine samples. Unreliability also stems from the tendency of drug screens to confuse similar chemical compounds. For example, codeine and Vicks Formula 44-M have been known to produce positive results for heroin, Advil for marijuana, and Nyquil for amphetamines.

American Civil Liberties Union, "Drug Testing in the Workplace," 1996.

It is clear from the concessions occasionally made by supporters of drug testing that their case remains shaky. "Only limited information is available about the actual effects of illicit drug use in the workplace," admits the Drug Free America Foundation on its Web site. "We do not have reliable data on the relative cost-effectiveness of various types of interventions within specific industries, much less across industries. Indeed, only a relatively few studies have attempted true cost/benefit evaluations of actual interventions, and these studies reflect that we are in only the very early stages of learning how to apply econometrics to these evaluations."

Lacking solid data, advocates of drug testing tend to rely on weak studies and bogus numbers. The Office of National

Drug Control Policy, for example, claims a 1995 study by Houston's Drug-Free Business Initiative "demonstrated that workplace drug testing reduces injuries and worker's compensation claims." Yet the study's authors noted that the "findings concerning organizational performance indicators are based on numbers of cases too small to be statistically meaningful. While they are informative and provide basis for speculation, they are not in any way definitive or conclusive, and should be regarded as hypotheses for future research."

Phantom Numbers

Sometimes the "studies" cited by promoters of drug testing do not even exist. Quest Diagnostics, a leading drug testing company, asserts on its Web site that "substance abusers" are "3.6 times more likely to be involved in on-the-job accidents" and "5 times more likely to file a worker's compensation claim." As Queens College sociologist Lynn Zimmer has shown, the original source of these numbers, sometimes identified as "the Firestone Study," was a 1972 speech to Firestone Tire executives in which an advocate of employee assistance programs compared workers with "medical-behavioral problems" to other employees. He focused on alcoholism, mentioning illegal drugs only in passing, and he cited no research to support his seemingly precise figures. Another number from the Firestone speech appears on the Web site of Roche Diagnostics, which claims "substance abusers utilize their medical benefits 300 percent more often than do their non-using co-workers."

Roche also tells employers that "the federal government estimates" that "the percentage of your workforce that has a substance abuse problem" is "about 17 percent." This claim appears to be a distortion of survey data collected by the National Institute of Mental Health (NIMH). As summarized by the American Psychiatric Association, the data indicate that "nearly 17 percent of the U.S. population 18 years old and over will fulfill criteria for alcohol or drug abuse in their lifetimes." By contrast, Roche is telling employers that 17 percent of the population meets the criteria at any given time. Furthermore, the vast majority of the drug abusers identified by the NIMH were alcoholics, so the number does not bolster the case for urinalysis aimed at catching illegal drug users.

According to a study published in February [2002] in the *Archives of General Psychiatry*, less than 8 percent of the adult population meets the criteria for "any substance use disorder" in a given year, and 86 percent of those cases involve alcohol. The study, based on data from the National Comorbidity Survey, found that 2.4 percent of respondents had a "substance use disorder" involving a drug other than alcohol in the previous year. So Roche's figure—which is also cited by other companies that profit from drug testing, such as RapidCup and eVeriTest—appears to be off by a factor of at least two and perhaps seven, depending upon whether "substance abuse problem" is understood to include alcohol.

Drinking Problems

This ambiguity seems to be deliberate. To magnify the size of the problem facing employers, the government and the drug testing industry routinely conflate illegal drugs with alcohol. But it's clear that employers are not expected to treat drinkers the way they treat illegal drug users. Although drinking is generally not allowed on company time, few employers do random tests to enforce that policy. In 1995, according to survey data collected by Tyler Hartwell and his colleagues, less than 14 percent of work sites randomly tested employees for alcohol. And while 22 percent tested applicants for alcohol, such tests do not indicate whether someone had a drink, say, the night before. In any case, it's a rare employer who refuses to hire drinkers.

When it comes to illegal drugs, by contrast, the rule is zero tolerance: Any use, light or heavy, on duty or off, renders an applicant or worker unfit for employment. "With alcohol, the question has always been not 'Do you consume?' but 'How much?'" notes Ted Shults, chairman of the American Association of Medical Review Officers, which trains and certifies physicians who specialize in drug testing. "With the illegal drugs, it's always, 'Did you use it?'"

The double standard is especially striking because irresponsible drinking is by far the biggest drug problem affecting the workplace. "Alcohol is the most widely abused drug among working adults," the U.S. Department of Labor notes. It cites an estimate from the Substance Abuse and Mental Health Services Administration that alcohol accounts for 86 percent of the costs imposed on businesses by drug abuse.

Drug Users Versus Drinkers

In part, the inconsistency reflects the belief that illegal drug users are more likely than drinkers to become addicted and to be intoxicated on the job. There is no evidence to support either assumption. The vast majority of pot smokers, like the vast majority of drinkers, are occasional or moderate users. About 12 percent of the people who use marijuana in a given year, and about 3 percent of those who have ever tried it, report smoking it on 300 or more days in the previous year. A 1994 study based on data from the National Comorbidity Survey estimated that 9 percent of marijuana users have ever met the American Psychiatric Association's criteria for "substance dependence." The comparable figure for alcohol was 15 percent.

According to the testing industry, however, any use of an illegal drug inevitably leads to abuse. "Can employees who use drugs be good workers?" Roche asks in one of its promotional documents. Its answer: "Perhaps, for a while. Then, with extended use and abuse of drugs and alcohol, their performance begins to deteriorate. They lose their edge. They're late for work more often or they miss work all together. . . .Suddenly, one person's drug problem becomes everyone's problem." This equation of use with abuse is a staple of prohibitionist propaganda. "It is simply not true," says the Drug-Free America Foundation, "that a drug user or alcohol abuser leaves his habit at the factory gate or the office door." The message is that a weekend pot smoker should be as big a worry as an employee who comes to work drunk every day.

Employers respond to the distinctions drawn by the government. Under the Americans with Disabilities Act, for example, alcoholics cannot be penalized or fired without evidence that their drinking is hurting their job performance. With illegal drugs, however, any evidence of use is sufficient grounds for disciplinary action or dismissal.

Periodical Bibliography

The following articles have been selected to supplement the diverse views presented in this chapter.

American Civil Liberties Union	"Drug Testing in the Workplace," 1996. www.aclu.org.
Mark Boal	"The Supreme Court vs. Teens," *Rolling Stone*, June 6, 2002.
Peter Cassidy	"Pee First, Ask Questions Later," *In These Times*, December 20, 2002.
Barbara Ehrenreich	"Your Urine, Please," *Progressive*, March 2000.
Frank Furedi	"Making a Virtue of Vice," *Spectator*, January 12, 2002.
Lawrence O. Gostin	"The Rights of Pregnant Women," *Hastings Center Report*, September/October 2001.
Walter Kirn	"Hidden Lessons," *New York Times Magazine*, April 14, 2002.
David Masci	"Preventing Teen Drug Use: Is the 'Get-Tough' Approach Effective?" *CQ Researcher*, March 15, 2002.
Nina Riccio	"To Test or Not to Test?" *Current Health*, March 2003.
David C. Slade	"Moms' Privacy Trumps Infants' Health," *World & I*, June 2001.
Welch Suggs	"Deadly Fuel: As Supplements and Steroids Tempt and Endanger More Athletes, What Are Colleges Doing?" *Chronicle of Higher Education*, March 14, 2003.
Jacob Sullum	"Free Will," *Reason*, May 2002.
Tom Verducci	"Five Strikes and You're Out . . . Maybe, Sort Of," *Sports Illustrated*, November 24, 2003.
Tom Verducci	"A Testy Issue," *Sports Illustrated*, June 3, 2002.
L. Jon Wertheim	"Taking Their Hits," *Sports Illustrated*, December 9, 2002.
Ryoko Yamaguchi, Lloyd D. Johnson, and Patrick M. O'Malley	"Relationship Between Student Illicit Drug Use and School Drug-Testing Policies," *Journal of School Health*, April 2003.

CHAPTER 4

How Can Drug Abuse Be Reduced?

Chapter Preface

While federal policy on drug abuse still views any type of illegal drug use a punishable crime, many state and local governments are beginning to relax their drug policies. For example, hundreds of local jurisdictions have decided to treat drug offenders instead of jailing them. Treatment programs are just one example of what have become known as "harm reduction" policies, which attempt to reduce the harms associated with using illegal drugs. Needle-exchange programs (NEPs) are another example of harm reduction policies.

Harm reduction is based on the belief that people have always used and will continue to use drugs. The basic aim behind harm reduction is to implement policies that will reduce the harmful consequences—to both users and society—of illegal drug use. Harm reduction programs first appeared in the United States in the 1980s during the AIDS epidemic, when scientists and researchers discovered that the AIDS virus (HIV) could be transmitted by the sharing of dirty needles. To help check the AIDS/HIV epidemic, public health workers began counseling drug injection users not to share their needles with other users, or, if they must share needles, to at least disinfect them with bleach between uses.

Some cities established needle-exchange programs in which users could exchange a used needle for a sterile one. Various public health agencies—including the Centers for Disease Control and Prevention, the American Public Health Association, the American Medical Association, the American Bar Association, and the National Academy of Sciences—all support needle-exchange programs. The organizations and their supporters claim that needle-exchange programs reduce the spread of AIDS without increasing drug use. The programs also serve as an outreach program for addicts, many of whom are convinced by professionals at needle-exchange clinics to enter drug treatment programs.

Opponents of needle-exchange programs argue that they are not an effective harm reduction policy, and in fact, just make it easier for addicts to continue abusing drugs instead of entering treatment programs. Barry McCaffrey, director of the Office of National Drug Control Policy during the

Clinton administration, argues that providing government funding for needle-exchange programs makes it appear as though the government sanctions illegal drug use. Other critics point out that most injection drug users do not die from AIDS but from overdoses and other health problems associated with drug use. They point to a review of twenty-one studies of needle-exchange programs revealing that the infection rate of HIV among injection drug users who used NEPs was no higher—and no lower—than those who did not. Herbert Kleber, a physician at Columbia University in New York, asserts, "NEPs may, in theory, be effective, but the data doesn't prove that they are."

Harm reduction policies continue to be hotly debated. The authors in the following chapter discuss other policies being implemented in an effort to reduce America's drug problems.

"Our current policies balancing prevention, enforcement, and treatment have kept drug usage outside the scope of acceptable behavior in the U.S."

The War on Drugs Reduces Drug Abuse

Asa Hutchinson

In the following viewpoint Asa Hutchinson contends that the war on drugs has not failed, but unlike real wars, it is a continual struggle that will never end. Hutchinson points out that the drug war is succeeding, as evidenced by the fact that fewer people are using drugs now than they were when the war on drugs first started. Hutchinson concludes that many new ideas are being tested in the war on drugs, but continuing to enforce tough laws against drug use is essential. Hutchinson is the former director of the Drug Enforcement Administration.

As you read, consider the following questions:

1. By what percentage is overall drug use down in the United States since the late 1970s, as cited by Hutchinson?
2. What percentage of the U.S. population uses illegal drugs, according to the author?
3. What percentage of drug felons sentenced to prison in New York were charged with sale or intent to sell, as cited by Hutchinson?

Asa Hutchinson, speech at the Modernizing Criminal Justice Conference, London, England, June 18, 2002.

It is a distinct privilege for this farm boy from Gravette, Arkansas, to be in the land where the principle of liberty secured by law became a foundation of all democratic societies. From the rights laid down in the Magna Carta to the institution of the writ of *habeas corpus*, we find in this land the very foundations of a free and just society.

In this century, Great Britain has continued to stand as a bulwark against tyranny. Both in World War II and now in our war against terrorism, England has been steadfast in support of freedom. I am grateful for the leadership of Prime Minister [Tony] Blair. He has defined the attacks against America very clearly as a battle between not just America and the terrorists, but between *all* of the free world and terrorism.

The War on Drugs

I am here to speak about another war today—the war on drugs. It is perhaps not as intriguing as the war on terrorism—but as we know—drug trafficking and terrorism are two evils that exist in the same jungle. They make a deadly combination like wind and fire that threatens our societies. For that reason, we cannot abandon nor weaken our resolve in this ongoing struggle.

The nations represented in this room understand the human suffering that comes with war. We know that war should be avoided, but not at the sacrifice of freedom. We know wars are fought to sustain democracy, but they are not without costs. We know that the costs of war must be weighed against what is lost when evil triumphs.

These realities of war are common in democratic societies. We know they are also true when it comes to our shared struggle against illegal drugs. If we avoid the war, then democracy will suffer; if we flinch at the costs, then a greater price will be paid by families, by communities, and by our nations.

It is because drug addictions weaken us and drug violence threatens the rule of law. Democracy cannot remain strong if our society succumbs to a culture of drugs that seeks to enslave, diminish, and corrupt the citizens. That is the reason we persist and remain vigilant in this fight.

The difficulty in the analogy of war is that we desire and

expect for war to end—either in victory or defeat. But we must understand that some wars reflect an on-going struggle. As long as there is temptation, despair, greed, and youthful indiscretion, there will be drug abuse. But each step of the way there will be victories marked by changed lives, less usage, and reduced availability of illegal drugs. Yes, it is an on-going struggle, but there is the reward of life-transforming human victories.

In many circles, U.S. drug policy is under attack. It is being criticized primarily by those who favor a legalization agenda. It is also being challenged by those who approve of the trends in Europe of decriminalization, harm reduction, and distinctions between hard and soft drugs.

I have had occasions to debate many of these proponents of a shift in U.S. drug policy. Invariably, the arguments for change are based upon misinformation and distortions of the real facts in the United States. The arguments for change are based upon 4 myths. Myths that have been perpetuated by those who seek change and myths that are believed by some because they have lost hope. Let me discuss and dispute each of these 4 myths.

A Miserable Failure?

#1: The first is that America's drug policy is a miserable failure.

The facts are just the contrary.

First, on the demand side. We've reduced casual use, chronic use, and prevented others from even starting. Overall drug use in the United States is down 50% since the late 1970s. That's 9.3 million people fewer using illegal drugs. We've reduced cocaine use by an astounding 75% during the last 15 years. That's 4 million people fewer using cocaine on a regular basis.

The crack cocaine epidemic of the 1980s and early 1990s has diminished in scope. And we've reduced the number of *chronic* heroin users over the last decade. And the number of new marijuana users and cocaine users continues to steadily decrease.

This is not to say we have done enough. We still have much progress to make. We are concerned with emerging drug threats like Ecstasy and methamphetamine. But the fact is that our current policies balancing prevention, enforcement, and treatment have kept drug usage outside the scope of acceptable behavior in the U.S.

To put it in perspective, less than 5% of the population uses illegal drugs of any kind. That's 12½ million regular users of all illegal drugs compared to 55 million tobacco users and over 100 million alcohol users.

Drug policy also has an impact on general crime. In a 2001 study, the British Home Office found violent crime and property crime increased in the late 1990s in every wealthy country except the United States. I know our murder rate is too high, and we have much to learn from those with greater success—but this reduction is due in part to a reduction in drug use.

On the supply side, we're having successes, too. And this is where the DEA [Drug Enforcement Administration] focuses much of our efforts: enforcement and interdiction. The goal is to *increase* the risks to traffickers and *decrease* drug availability.

For example: The increased law enforcement presence at the U.S.-Mexico border since [the September 11, 2001, terrorist attacks] has resulted in increased drug seizures. Customs officials seized more than 16,000 pounds of cocaine along the border in the [first half of 2002], almost twice as much as the same period [in the previous] year. At one of our ports in Texas, seizures of methamphetamine are up 425% and heroin by 172%. Enforcement makes a difference—traffickers' costs go up with these kind of seizures.

The new Office of Homeland Security President [George W.] Bush is creating will make our border interdiction even more productive by coordinating efforts more effectively. There has been success, and the reports of failure are only myths.

Prisons and Drug Users

#2: The second myth is that U.S. prisons are filled with drug users.

There is a perception that law enforcement in the United States targets drug users and that our prisons are filled with those who possess small amounts of drugs.

On the contrary, only 5% of people in U.S. *federal* prisons for drug offenses are there on possession convictions. In our *state* prisons, it's somewhat higher—about 27% of drug offenders.

But from my experience as a federal prosecutor, most of those in prison on possession charges are traffickers who plea bargained down to a possession charge, or are people with repeat offenses. The fact is, you have to work pretty hard to end up in jail for drug possession in the United States.

The Drug War Has Not Failed

History shows that, far from being a failure, drug-control programs are among the most successful public-policy efforts of the later half of the 20th century. According to a national drug survey, between 1979 and 1992, the most intense period of antidrug efforts, the rate of illegal drug use dropped by more than half, while marijuana use decreased by two-thirds. Cocaine use dropped by three-fourths between 1985 and 1992.

Why is this record described as a failure?

William J. Bennett, *Opinion Journal*, May 15, 2001.

In New York, which has received criticism from some because of its tough Rockefeller drug laws, it is estimated that 97% of drug felons sentenced to prison were charged with sale or intent to sell.

In fact, first time drug offenders, even sellers, typically do not go to prison.

In addition, there has been a shift in the U.S. criminal justice system to provide treatment for nonviolent felons with addiction problems, rather than incarceration. In New York, prosecutors currently divert from prison each year over 7,000 convicted drug felons. Many enter treatment programs. In fact, the criminal justice system acts as the largest referral source for drug treatment programs.

I hope the 2nd myth that users fill our prisons has been dispelled.

A Harmless Drug?

#3: The third myth is that cannabis is a harmless drug and therefore should be excluded from the anti-drug effort.

Drug legalization advocates in the United States single out cannabis as a different kind of drug, unlike cocaine and heroin and methamphetamine. They say it's less dangerous. And I know some countries in Europe have lowered its classification.

But in the United States, there's a growing number of people who are not finding marijuana quite as harmless as the myth claims.

In 1999, a record 225,000 Americans entered substance abuse treatment primarily for marijuana dependence. It's second only to heroin—and not by much. In addition, 87,000 people sought treatment at hospital emergency rooms for medical problems related to marijuana—about the same as those for heroin-related problems.

Clearly, cannabis causes health problems and dependence. It impacts young people's mental development, their ability to concentrate in school, and their motivation and initiative to reach goals.

And, like all drugs, cannabis harms far more than the user: A study in the United States showed that as many car accidents were caused by drivers using marijuana as were caused by alcohol. Of adult males arrested for all kinds of crime, 40% of them tested positive for marijuana at the time of their arrest.

If we are to effectively confront drug problems in our society, we cannot accept the myth that marijuana represents no harm. It does.

Innovative Ideas in the Drug War

#4: The fourth, and final, myth is that there are no new ideas in the fight against drugs.

There are many innovative ideas in American drug policy—ideas that are achieving success. From drug courts to community coalitions; from more investment in education to more effective treatment; from drug testing in the workplace to drug counselors in schools, these are ideas that work.

Enforcement is necessary because it puts a risk in trafficking and sets the right social parameters for behavior in our country. But enforcement alone is not going to do the job. It takes education to teach young people to make the right decisions in life, and it takes treatment to heal those who have become addicted. The Bush Administration is investing more in prevention and treatment efforts than ever before—we've increased funding for those efforts by almost a quarter from 1999. For just treatment alone, we've budgeted $3 billion—a 27% increase. Also, substance abuse research is funded at record levels.

One of the most successful new ideas in our country is drug courts. In the United States, we've got 600 in operation, with plans to greatly expand because of their tremendous success. Through close supervision and monitoring by the court, nonviolent drug offenders are overcoming drug addiction. Drug courts offer treatment with accountability. And it's one of the most important things we're doing in the anti-drug effort.

New Ideas Are Essential

Another new idea we initiated at the DEA is an Integrated Drug Enforcement Assistance program. We call it IDEA. With this program, we give lasting impact to drug enforcement operations. The DEA takes pride in removing criminal organizations from neighborhoods. But if the demand remains and the culture of the community has not changed, then another trafficking organization takes over.

That's frustrating to law enforcement. With the IDEA program, our approach is to dismantle the criminal organizations, but at the same time work side-by-side with community coalitions to dry up the demand. We're working with schools, civic groups, businesses, churches, and health professionals to change the character of the community.

New ideas are essential in working old problems. But these new ideas should be within the framework that drugs are illegal and there should be risk and accountability for use.

So those are 4 often repeated views about U.S. drug policy, and they are all myths. They're dangerous beliefs because people draw a faulty conclusion from them: that we need to abandon current drug policy. That drugs need to be decriminalized, legalized, or somehow managed.

We need to aim higher than simply managing drug addicts. Maintaining addictions will never bring down demand.

Decriminalizing classes of drugs weakens the message that drug abuse is harmful.

In deciding where to go with drug policy, we have the responsibility to look at the facts, dispel the myths, and make progress.

A Problem for a Long Time

That progress doesn't come overnight. But it will come. America has had a long problem with drugs. It's not a war we've been fighting for 20 years. We've been fighting it for 120 years. In 1880, many drugs, including opium and cocaine, were legal. We didn't know their harms, but we soon learned. We saw the highest level of drug use ever in our nation, per capita. There were over 400,000 opium addicts in our nation. That's twice as many per capita as there are today. And like today, we saw rising crime with that drug abuse.

But we fought those problems by passing and enforcing tough laws. And they worked—by World War II, drug use was reduced to the very margins of society. And ever since then, we've looked to our drug laws to teach us acceptable parameters of behavior. We look to our laws to uphold standards of accountability. The fact is—it is our laws that keep the vast majority of our citizens away from drugs.

And that is our responsibility as government leaders. Let me conclude by quoting Winston Churchill—a great lover of freedom. He said that, "The price of greatness is responsibility." Yes, all of our great nations have that responsibility to take us in a direction that will reject permissive drug abuse and drug dependence. A direction that will take the next generation to an even greater future. A future that upholds the rule of law and gives hope through the just enforcement of our laws.

> "*Our drug war has done little more than push drug cultivation from one region to the next while drugs on our streets have become cheaper, purer, and more plentiful than ever.*"

The War on Drugs Does Not Reduce Drug Abuse

Sanho Tree

Sanho Tree is a fellow and director of the Drug Policy Project at the Institute for Policy Studies in Washington, D.C. In the following viewpoint Tree argues that draconian law enforcement efforts do not solve the problem of drug abuse, and, in fact, only make it worse. Tree contends that the war on drugs has had the opposite effect intended; by constricting the supply of illegal drugs and jailing the inept and inefficient traffickers, profits have skyrocketed for the smarter dealers left behind. The solution, Tree maintains, is to find ways to minimize the harm caused by illegal drugs.

As you read, consider the following questions:
1. U.S. prisoners make up what percentage of the world's entire prison population, according to Tree?
2. What is the unique budgetary logic used to support increased funding for the war on drugs, as cited by the author?
3. How does the philosophy of "harm reduction" allow the United States to manage the drug abuse problem, in Tree's opinion?

Sanho Tree, "The War at Home," *Sojourners*, May/June 2003. Copyright © 2003 by *Sojourners*. Reproduced by permission. (800) 714-7474, www.sojo.net.

In 1965, Sen. Robert F. Kennedy tried to promote an enlightened drug policy before our country declared war on its own citizens. He told Congress, "Now, more than at any other time in our history, the addict is a product of a society which has moved faster and further than it has allowed him to go, a society which in its complexity and its increasing material comfort has left him behind. In taking up the use of drugs the addict is merely exhibiting the outermost aspects of a deep-seated alienation from this society, of a combination of personal problems having both psychological and sociological aspects."

Kennedy continued, "The fact that addiction is bound up with the hard core of the worst problems confronting us socially makes it discouraging at the outset to talk about 'solving' it. 'Solving' it really means solving poverty and broken homes, racial discrimination and inadequate education, slums and unemployment. . . ." Thirty-eight years later, the preconditions contributing to drug addiction have changed little, but our response to the problem has become overwhelmingly punitive.

Law Enforcement Responses

When confronted with illegal behavior, legislators have traditionally responded by escalating law enforcement. Yet countries such as Iran and China that routinely use the death penalty for drug offenses still have serious drug problems. Clearly there are limits to what can be achieved through coercion. By treating this as a criminal justice problem, our range of solutions has been sharply limited: How much coercion do we need to make this problem go away? No country has yet found that level of repression, and it is unlikely many Americans would want to live in a society that did.

As the drug war escalated in the 1980s, mandatory minimum sentencing and other Draconian penalties boosted our prison population to unprecedented levels. With more than 2 million people behind bars (there are only 8 million prisoners in the entire world), the United States—with one–twenty-second of the world's population—has one-quarter of the planet's prisoners. We operate the largest penal system in the world, and approximately one-quarter of all our prisoners (nearly half a million people) are there for nonviolent drug offenses—that's more drug prisoners than the entire European Union incarcerates for all offenses combined, and the EU has over 90 million more citizens than the United States. Put another way, the United States now has more nonviolent drug prisoners alone than we had in our entire prison population in 1980.

If the drug war were evaluated like most other government programs, we would have tried different strategies long ago. But our current policy seems to follow its own unique budgetary logic. A slight decline in drug use is used as evidence that our drug war is finally starting to work and therefore we should ramp up the funding. But a rise in drug use becomes proof that we are not doing enough to fight drugs and must therefore redouble our efforts and really ramp up the funding. Under this unsustainable dynamic, funding and incarceration rates can only ratchet upward. When [Richard] Nixon won reelection in 1972, the annual federal drug war budget was approximately $100 million. Now it is approaching $20 billion. Our legislators have been paralyzed by the doctrine of "if at first you don't succeed, escalate."

Internationally, our drug war has done little more than push drug cultivation from one region to the next while drugs on our streets have become cheaper, purer, and more plentiful than ever. Meanwhile, the so-called collateral damage from our international drug war has caused incalculable suffering to peasant farmers caught between the crossfire of our eradication policies and the absolute lack of economic alternatives that force them to grow illicit drug crops to feed their families. Unable to control our own domestic demand, our politicians have lashed out at other peoples for daring to feed our seemingly insatiable craving for these substances. We have exported our failures and scapegoated others.

Fears of Being Seen as "Soft on Drugs"

Many legislators approve increased drug war funding because they are true believers that cracking down is the only way to deal with unlawful conduct. Others support it out of ignorance that alternative paradigms exist. But perhaps most go along with the drug war for fear of being depicted as "soft on drugs" in negative campaign ads at election time.

In recent years, there has been an increasingly lively debate on whether nonviolent drug offenders should receive treatment or incarceration. As legislators gradually drift toward funding more badly needed treatment slots, an important dynamic of the drug economy is still left out of the national debate: the economics of prohibition. Elected officials and much of the media have been loath to discuss this phenomenon at the risk of being discredited as a "legalizer," but until a solution is found concerning this central issue, many of the societal problems concerning illicit drugs will continue to plague us. Trying to find a sustainable solution to manage the drug problem without discussing the consequences of prohibition is like taking one's car to the mechanic for repair but not allowing the hood to be opened. The time has come to take a look under the hood of our unwinnable drug war.

Worthless Weeds

Under a prohibition economy where there is high demand, escalating law enforcement often produces the opposite of the intended result. By attempting to constrict supply while demand remains high, our policies have made these relatively worthless commodities into substances of tremendous value. The alchemists of the Middle Ages tried in vain for centuries to find a formula to turn lead into gold, but it took our drug warriors to perfect the new alchemy of turning worthless weeds into virtual gold. Some varieties of the most widely used illicit drug, marijuana, are now worth their weight in solid gold (around $350 per ounce). Cocaine and heroin are worth many, many times their equivalent weight in gold. In a world filled with tremendous poverty, greed, and desire, we cannot make these substances disappear by making them more valuable.

Another factor we have failed to take into account is the virtually inexhaustible reservoir of impoverished peasants who will risk growing these crops in the vast regions of the world where these plants can flourish. According to the UN Development Program and the World Bank, there are 1.2 billion people in the world who live on less than $1 a day.

Imagine paying for housing, food, clothing, education, transportation, fertilizer, and medicine on less than $1 a day. Now imagine the temptation of putting a worthless seed into the soil and coming up with an illicit crop that can mean the difference between simple poverty or slow starvation for you and your family. We cannot escalate the value of such commodities through prohibition and not expect desperately poor farmers to plant any crop necessary to ensure their survival.

The Law of Supply and Demand

Of all the laws that Congress can pass or repeal, the law of supply and demand is not one of them. Neither is the law of evolution nor the law of unintended consequences. The drug trade evolves under Darwinian principles—survival of the fittest. Our response of increasing law enforcement ensures that the clumsy and inefficient traffickers are weeded out while the smarter and more adaptable ones tend to escape. We cannot hope to win a war on drugs when our policies see to it that only the most efficient drug operations survive. Indeed, these survivors are richly rewarded because we have constricted just enough supply to increase prices and profits while "thinning out the herd" by eliminating their competition for them. Through this process of artificial selection, we have been unintentionally breeding "super traffickers" for decades. Our policy of attacking the weakest links has caused tremendous human suffering, wasted countless lives and resources, and produced highly evolved criminal operations.

Our policy of applying a "war" paradigm to fight drug abuse and addiction betrays a gross ignorance of the dimensions of this medical problem and its far-reaching social and economic consequences. Wars employ brute force to extract political concessions from rational state actors. Drugs are articles of commerce that do not respond to fear, pain, or congressional dictates. However, around these crops revolve hundreds of thousands, indeed millions, of individuals responding to the artificially inflated value of these essentially worthless agricultural products. For every trafficker that our "war" manages to stop, a dozen others take his or her place because individuals—whether acting out of poverty, greed, or addiction—enter the drug economy on the assumption they won't get caught, and most never are. No "war" can elicit a unified political capitulation from actors in such diverse places as Southeast Asia, the Andes, suburbia, and the local street corner. Such a war can never be won, but a "harm reduction" approach offers ways to contain and manage the problem.

A Policy That Solves Nothing

Guns and helicopters cannot solve the problems of poverty in the Andes or addiction in the United States. Moreover, our policies of employing more police, prosecutors, and prisons to deal with the drug problem is like digging more graves to solve the global AIDS pandemic—it solves nothing. As sociologist Craig Reinarman notes, our policies attack the symptoms but do little to address the underlying problems. "Drugs are richly functional scapegoats," Reinarman writes. "They provide elites with fig leafs to place over the unsightly social ills that are endemic to the social system over which they preside. They provide the public with a restricted aperture of attribution in which only the chemical bogey man or lone deviant come into view and the social causes of a cornucopia of complex problems are out of the picture."

Until we provide adequate resources for drug treatment, rehabilitation, and prevention, the United States will continue to consume billions of dollars worth of drugs and impoverished peasants around the world will continue to grow them. The enemy is not an illicit agricultural product that can be grown all over the world; rather, our policies should be directed against poverty, despair, and alienation. At home and abroad, these factors drive the demand for illicit drugs which is satisfied by an inexhaustible reservoir of impoverished peasant farmers who have few other economic options with which to sustain themselves and their families.

Some day, there will be a just peace in Colombia and a humane drug control policy in the United States. Until then, we are mortgaging the future, and the most powerless among us must pay most of the interest. That interest can be seen in the faces of the *campesinos* [farmworkers] and indigenous peoples caught in the crossfire of our Andean drug war; it can be seen in the millions of addicts in the United States who cannot get treatment they need; it can be seen in the prisons filled with nonviolent drug offenders; and it can be seen in the poverty, despair, and alienation around the world because we choose to squander our resources on harmful programs while ignoring the real needs of the dispossessed.

A Steady Flow of Drugs

The supply of drugs has not been hampered in any serious way by the war on drugs. A commission on federal law-enforcement practices chaired by former FBI director William Webster recently offered this blunt assessment of the interdiction efforts: "Despite a record number of seizures and a flood of legislation, the Commission is not aware of any evidence that the flow of narcotics into the United States has been reduced." Perhaps the most dramatic evidence of the failure of the drug war is the flourishing of open-air drug markets in Washington, D.C.—the very city in which the drug czar and the Drug Enforcement Administration have their headquarters.

Timothy Lynch, *After Prohibition*, 2000.

Because we have witnessed the damage illicit drugs can cause, we have allowed ourselves to fall prey to one of the great myths of the drug warriors: Keeping drugs illegal will protect us. But drug prohibition doesn't mean we control drugs, it means we give up the right to control them. Under prohibition, the people who control drugs are by definition criminals—and, very often, organized crime. We have made a deliberate choice not to regulate these drugs and have been paying the price for the anarchy that followed. These are lessons we failed to learn from our disastrous attempt at alcohol prohibition in the 1920s.

A Harm Reduction Approach

On the other hand, the philosophy of "harm reduction" offers us a way to manage the problem. Briefly put, this means we accept the premise that mind altering substances have always been part of human society and will not disappear, but we must find ways to minimize the harm caused by these substances while simultaneously minimizing the harm caused by the drug war itself. We have reached the point where the drug war causes more harm than the drugs themselves—which is the definition of a bankrupt policy. Drug abuse and addiction are medical problems, not criminal justice problems, and we should act accordingly.

Some examples of harm reduction include comprehensive and holistic drug treatment for addicts who ask for it, overdose prevention education, clean needle exchange to reduce the spread of HIV and hepatitis, methadone maintenance for heroin addicts, and honest prevention and education programs instead of the ineffective DARE [Drug Abuse Resistance Education] program.

We already know what doesn't work—the current system doesn't work—but we are not allowed to discover what eventually will work. Our current policy of doing more of the same is doomed to failure because escalating a failed paradigm will not produce a different result. However, by approaching the problem as managers rather than moralizers, we can learn from our mistakes and make real progress. It is our current system of the drug war that is the obstacle to finding an eventual workable system of drug control.

> "*Under a legalized scenario, we would see the level of drug use remain the same or decline. . . . The same would happen with respect to drug abuse.*"

Illicit Drugs Should Be Legalized

Gary E. Johnson

In the following viewpoint Gary E. Johnson argues that if illicit drugs were legalized, rates of drug use and abuse would stay level or decline. He contends that legalizing drugs would enable the government to control, regulate, and tax them, leading to a healthier society. According to Johnson, most Americans no longer support the war on drugs and would approve of a drug legalization scheme. Gary E. Johnson is the former governor of New Mexico.

As you read, consider the following questions:
1. What new drug laws does Johnson describe?
2. According to the author, how many marijuana-related arrests were there in 1997?
3. How does Johnson define drug legalization?

Gary E. Johnson, "It's Time to Legalize Drugs," *After Prohibition: An Adult Approach to Drug Policies in the 21st Century*, edited by Timothy Lynch. Washington, DC: Cato Institute, 2000.

I am a cost-benefit analysis person. What's the cost and what's the benefit? A couple of things scream out as failing cost-benefit criteria. One is education. The other is the war on drugs. We are presently spending $50 billion a year on the war on drugs. I'm talking about police, courts, and jails. For all the money that we're putting into the war on drugs, it is an absolute failure. The "outrageous" hypothesis that I have been raising is that under a legalized scenario, we could actually hold drug use level or see it decline. I realize that is arguable. But with respect to drug abuse, I don't think you can argue about that. Under a legalized scenario, we would see the level of drug use remain the same or decline. And the same would happen with respect to drug abuse.

Sometimes people say to me, "Governor, I am absolutely opposed to your stand on drugs." I respond by asking them, "You're for drugs, you want to see kids use drugs?" Let me make something clear. I'm not pro-drug. I'm against drugs. Don't do drugs. Drugs are a real handicap. Don't do alcohol. Don't do tobacco. They are a real handicap.

A New Set of Laws

There's another issue beyond cost-benefit criteria. Should you go to jail for using drugs? And I'm not talking about doing drugs and committing a crime or doing drugs and driving a car. Should you go to jail for simply doing drugs? I say no. I say that you shouldn't. People ask me, "What do you tell kids?" Well, you tell them the truth, that's what you tell them. You tell them that by legalizing drugs, we can control them, regulate them, and tax them. If we legalize drugs, we might have a healthier society. And you explain to them how that might take place. But you tell them that drugs are a bad choice. Don't do drugs. But if you do drugs, we're not going to throw you in jail for that.

Under a legalized scenario, I say there is going to be a whole new set of laws. Let me just mention a few of those new laws. Let's say you can't do drugs if you're under 21 years of age. You can't sell drugs to kids. I say employers should be able to discriminate against drug users. Employers should be able to conduct drug tests and they should not have to comply with the Americans With Disabilities Act.

Do drugs and do crime? Make it like a gun. Enhance the penalty for the crime in the same way we do today with guns. Do drugs and drive? There should be a law similar to the law we have now for driving under the influence of alcohol.

I am proposing that we redirect the $50 billion that we're presently spending (state and federal) on the old set of laws to enforce a new set of laws. I sense a new society out there when you're talking about enforcing these new laws and enhancing the ability of law enforcement to focus on other crimes that are being committed. Police can crack down on speeding violations, burglaries, and other crimes that law enforcement does not have the opportunity to enforce.

Under a legalized scenario, there will be a new set of problems. And we can all point them out. We can talk all day about the new set of problems that will accompany legalization. But I suggest to you that the new problems are going to be about half the negative consequence of what we've got today. A legalization model will be a dynamic process that will be fine-tuned as we go along.

Locking Up Americans Because of Bad Choices

I recall when I was in high school in 1971. An Albuquerque police officer came in, lit up some marijuana weeds and said, "If you smell this, run. This is marijuana and you need to know that if you do marijuana, we're going to catch you and we're going to put you in jail." I remember raising my hand at that time, asking, "What are you going to do, put 15 million people in jail?" The police officer said, "I don't care about that. I just care about the fact that if you do it, we're going to catch you and we're going to put you in jail." I'm afraid that prophecy may be coming true. In 1997 there were about 700,000 arrests for marijuana-related offenses.

Does anybody want to press a button that would retroactively punish the 80 million Americans who have done illegal drugs over the years? I might point out that I'm one of those individuals. In running for my first term in office, I offered up the fact that I had smoked marijuana. And the media was very quick to say, "Oh, so you experimented with marijuana?" "No," I said, "I *smoked* marijuana!" This is something that I did. I did it along with a lot of other people.

I look back on it now and I view drugs as a handicap. I stopped because it was a handicap. The same with drinking and tobacco. But did my friends and I belong in jail? I don't think that we should continue to lock up Americans because of bad choices.

Marijuana Versus Alcohol

And what about the bad choices regarding alcohol and tobacco? I've heard people say, "Governor, you're not comparing alcohol to drugs? You're not comparing tobacco to drugs?" I say, "*Hell no!*" Alcohol killed 150,000 people [in 1999]. And I'm not talking about drinking and driving. I'm just talking about the health effects. The health effects of tobacco killed 450,000 people [in 1999]. I don't mean to be flippant, but I don't know of anybody who ever died from a marijuana overdose. I'm sure there are a few that smoked enough marijuana to probably die from it. I'm sure that that's the case. I understand that 2,000 to 3,000 people died [in 1999] from cocaine and heroin. Under a legalized scenario, theoretically speaking, those deaths go away. Those don't become accidental deaths anymore. They become suicides, because we'd be talking about a legalized scenario where drugs will be controlled, where drugs will be taxed, where we would have education to go along with it. I want to be so bold as to say that marijuana is never going to have the devastating effects on society that alcohol has had on us.

My own informal poll among doctors is that 75 to 80 percent of people that doctors examine have health-related problems due to alcohol and tobacco. My brother is a cardio-thoracic surgeon, performing heart transplants. My brother says that 80 percent of the problems that he sees are alcohol and tobacco related. He says he sees about six people a year who have infected heart valves because of intravenous drug use, but the infection isn't from the drugs themselves. It's the dirty needles that cause the health problems.

Marijuana is said to be a gateway drug. We all know that, right? You're 85 times more likely to do cocaine if you do marijuana. I don't mean to be flippant, but 100 percent of all substance abuse starts with milk. You've heard it, but that bears repeating. My new mantra here is "Just Say Know."

Just know that there are two sides to all these arguments. I think the facts boil down to drugs being a bad choice. Drugs are a handicap. But should someone go to jail for just doing drugs? That is the reality of what is happening today. I believe the time has come for that to end.

Legalization, Not Decriminalization

I've been talking about legalization and not decriminalization. Legalization means we educate, regulate, tax, and control the estimated $400 billion a year drug industry. That's larger than the automobile industry. Decriminalization is a muddy term. It turns its back to half the problems that we're facing—which is to get the entire economy of drugs above the line. So that's why I talk about legalization, meaning control, the ability to tax, the ability to regulate, and the ability to educate.

Myths About Legalization

Advocates of maintaining the status quo regarding our drug laws view any consideration toward legalization as heresy. Legalization would lead to rampant drug abuse among our citizens, hampering our nation with enormous social problems as sober-minded people rush out to become heroin addicts.

This is highly debatable (how many of your friends and neighbors are anxiously awaiting the chance to buy heroin but abstain simply because it's illegal?). . . .

For many people, legalization conjures up images of open-air drug festivals in which the same thugs operating in the black market are free to prowl around grade schools with no fear of prosecution. But legalization does not mean that all the laws are wiped off the books leading to a general free-for-all. Quite the opposite, in fact. Legalization allows us to introduce all sorts of controls over a market where we now have no control at all.

Arthur Cole, *San Diego Union-Tribune*, May 28, 2000.

We need to make drugs a controlled substance just like alcohol. Perhaps we ought to let the government regulate it; let the government grow it; let the government manufacture it, distribute it, market it; and if that doesn't lead to decreased drug use, I don't know what would!

Kids today will tell you that legal prescription drugs are

harder to come by than illegal drugs. Well, of course. To get legal drugs, you must walk into a pharmacy and show identification. It's the difference between a controlled substance and an illegal substance. A teenager today will tell you that a bottle of beer is harder to come by than a marijuana joint. That's where we've come to today. It's where we've come to with regard to controlling alcohol, but it shows how out of control drugs have become.

A legalization scenario isn't going to be like the end of alcohol prohibition. When Prohibition ended, there were advertisements on the radio right away that said, "Hey! Drink and be merry. It's cool." I don't see this like tobacco, where for so long we saw advertisements that said, "Hey! Smoking is good for your health." There are constitutional questions, but I envision advertising campaigns that discourage drug use. I don't see today's advertising campaigns as being honest, and that's part of the problem.

Telling the Truth

We need to have an honest educational campaign about drugs. The Partnership for a Drug Free America was bragging to me that it was responsible for the "Here's your brain, and here's your brain on drugs" ad. Well, some kids believe that, perhaps three-year-olds, maybe some nine- or ten-year-olds. But at some point, kids have friends that smoke marijuana for the first time. Like everybody else, I was also told that if you smoke marijuana, you're going to go crazy. You're going to do crime. You're going to lose your mind. Then you smoked marijuana for the first time and none of those things happened. Actually, it was kind of nice. And then you realized that they weren't telling you the truth. That's why I envision advertising that tells the truth, which says drugs are kind of nice and that's the lure of drugs. But the reality is that if you continue to do drugs, they are a real handicap.

"Drug Czar" Barry McCaffrey has made me his poster child for drug legalization. He claims that drug use has been cut in half and that we are winning the drug war. Well, let's assume that we have cut it in half. I don't buy that for a minute, but let's assume that it's true. Let's assume that drug use has, in fact, dropped in half. Well, if it has, in the late

1970s we were spending a billion dollars federally on the drug war. Today, the feds are spending $19 billion a year on the drug war. In the late 1970s, we were arresting a few hundred thousand people. Today, we're arresting 1.6 million people. Does that mean that as drug use declines (according to McCaffrey, it has declined by half) we're going to be spending $36 billion federally and that we're going to be arresting 3.2 million people annually? I mean, to follow that logic, when we're left with a few hundred users nationwide, we're going to be spending the entire gross national product on drug law enforcement!

I think it would be interesting to see some push polling done on the issue of drugs in this country. In other words, if the following is true, then how do you feel about "x"? If the following is true, how do you feel about "y"? But the questions that get asked today, I really feel like I understand the answers. People have been conditioned to believe that drugs are dangerous. The polls should ask, "Should you go to jail for just using drugs?" People overwhelmingly say no. But ask the question, "Should you go to jail for pushing drugs?" people say yes. People don't understand the profile of a pusher. Most people don't understand, as we New Mexicans do, that "mules" are carrying the drugs in. I'm talking about Mexican citizens who are paid a couple of hundred dollars to bring drugs across the border, and they don't even know who has given them the money. They just know that it's a king's ransom and that there are more than enough Mexican citizens willing to do that. The federal government is catching many of the mules, but the arrests are not making a difference in our war on drugs. We are catching some kingpins. Let's not deny that. But those that are caught, those links out of the chain, don't make any difference in the overall war on drugs.

"Right On!"

I want to tell you a little bit about the response that I've been getting to this, the response to what I've been saying. Politically, this is a zero. This is absolutely a zero. Politically, for anybody holding office, for anybody that aspires to hold office, for anybody who's held office, or for anybody who has a job associated with politics, this is verboten. I am in the ground, and the dirt is being thrown on top of my coffin. But what I want to tell you is that among the public, this is absolutely overwhelming. I suggest to you that this is the biggest head-in-the-sand issue that exists in this country today. In New Mexico, I am being approached rapid fire with people saying "right on" with your statements regarding the war on drugs. And I want to suggest to you that it's a 97-to-3 difference among the public. This has been unbelievable. To give you one example, two elderly ladies came up to my table during dinner the other night, Gertrude and Mabel. They said, "We're teachers and we just think your school voucher idea sucks. But your position on the war on drugs . . . Right on! Right on!"

"Legalization, by removing penalties and reducing price, would increase drug demand."

Illicit Drugs Should Not Be Legalized

John P. Walters

John P. Walters is the director of the Office of National Drug Control Policy. In the following viewpoint Walters argues that legalizing drugs is not the panacea for social and criminal ills that its supporters claim. Walters argues that since legal, prescription drugs pose dangers to those who abuse them, legalizing currently illicit drugs would obviously not eliminate the dangers of drug abuse. Legalizing drugs, he contends, would merely increase drug use and its attendant ills.

As you read, consider the following questions:

1. What reasons do advocates of legalization give to support their argument that illicit drugs should be legalized, as cited by Walters?
2. Why would legalizing drugs increase demand, according to the author?
3. How many heroin addicts did Great Britain have before and after physicians were permitted to prescribe the drug, as cited by Walters?

John P. Walters, "Don't Legalize Drugs," *Wall Street Journal*, July 19, 2002. Copyright © 2002 by Dow Jones & Company, Inc. Reproduced by permission.

The charge that "nothing works" in the fight against illegal drugs has led some people to grasp at an apparent solution: legalize drugs. They will have taken false heart from news from Britain where the government acted to downgrade the possession of cannabis to the status of a non-arrestable offense.

The Argument for Legalization

According to the logic of the legalizers, it's laws against drug use, not the drugs themselves, that do the greatest harm. The real problem, according to them, is not that the young use drugs, but that drug laws distort supply and demand. Violent cartels arise, consumers overpay for a product of unknown quality, and society suffers when the law restrains those who "harm no one but themselves."

Better, the argument goes, for the government to control the trade in narcotics. That should drive down the prices (heroin would be "no more expensive than lettuce," argues one proponent), eliminate violence, provide tax revenue, reduce prison crowding, and foster supervised injection facilities.

An Unrealistic Analogy

Sounds good. But is it realistic? The softest spot in this line of reasoning is the analogy with alcohol abuse. The argument goes roughly like this: "Alcohol is legal. Alcohol can be abused. Therefore, cocaine should be legal." Their strongest argument, by contrast, is that prohibition produces more costs than benefits, while legalized drugs provide more benefits than costs.

But legalizers overstate the social costs of prohibition, just as they understate the social costs of legalization. Take the statistic that more than 1.5 million Americans are arrested every year for drug crimes. Legalizers would have us believe that otherwise innocent people are being sent to prison (displacing "true" criminals) for merely toking up. But only a fraction of these arrestees are ever sentenced to prison. And there should be little question that most of those sentenced have earned their place behind bars.

Some 24% of state prison drug offenders are violent recidivists, while 83% have prior criminal histories. Only 17%

are in prison for "first time offenses," while nominal "low-level" offenders are often criminals who plea-bargain to escape more serious charges. The reality is that a high percentage of all criminals, regardless of the offense, use drugs. In New York, 79% of those arrested for any crime tested positive for drugs.

Causing Problems

First, legalizing illegal drugs will cause the same problems the U.S. has with legal drugs (e.g. alcohol, tobacco), but possibly worse. Most obviously, legal drugs will increase the number of drug addicts. There are already reports by the Drug Enforcement Administration (DEA) that illustrate the connection of historical crack epidemics to low-priced doses and how it increases drug use. Logically then, legalization would increase the number of marijuana, cocaine and heroin addicts to a degree that they will equal current numbers of cigarette smokers and alcoholics.

Moreover, legalization would not lead to a decrease in drug-related violence. If anything, there is a chance that it would increase crime, when considering that drug-related violence is not necessarily related to the drug trade. Even if legalization decreases drug trade and economic violence, the level of violence committed by those under the influence of drugs would be more frequent.

Steve Park, *Johns Hopkins News-Letter*, April 12, 2001.

Drug abuse alone cost an estimated $55 billion in 1998 (excluding criminal justice costs), and deaths directly related to drug use have more than doubled since 1980. Would increasing this toll make for a healthier America? Legalization, by removing penalties and reducing price, would increase drug demand. Make something easier and cheaper to obtain, and you increase the number of people who will try it. Legalizers love to point out that the Dutch decriminalized marijuana in 1976, with little initial impact. But as drugs gained social acceptance, use increased consistently and sharply, with a 300% rise in use by 1996 among 18–20 year-olds.

Britain, too, provides an instructive example. When British physicians were allowed to prescribe heroin to certain addicts, the number skyrocketed. From 68 British addicts in the program in 1960, the problem exploded to an estimated 20,000 heroin users in London alone by 1982.

More Questions than Answers

The idea that we can "solve" our complex drug problem by simply legalizing drugs raises more questions than it answers. For instance, what happens to the citizenship of those legally addicted? Will they have their full civil rights, such as voting? Can they be employed as school bus drivers? Nurses? What of a woman, legally addicted to cocaine, who becomes pregnant? Should she be constrained by the very government that provides for her habit?

Won't some addicts seek larger doses than those medically prescribed? Or seek to profit by selling their allotment to others, including minors? And what about those promised tax revenues—how do they materialize? As it is, European drug clinics aren't filled with productive citizens, but rather with demoralized zombies seeking a daily fix. Won't drugs become a disability entitlement?

Will legalization eliminate violence? The *New England Journal of Medicine* reported in 1999 on the risks for women injured in domestic violence. The most striking factor was a partner who used cocaine, which increased risk more than four times. That violence is associated not with drug laws, but with the drug. A 1999 report from the Department of Health and Human Services showed that two million children live with a parent who has a drug problem. Studies indicate that up to 80% of our child welfare caseload involves caregivers who abuse substances. Drug users do not harm only themselves.

Laws Are Not the Problem

Legalizers like to argue that government-supervised production and distribution of addictive drugs will eliminate the dangers attributed to drug prohibition. But when analyzing this "harm reduction" argument, consider the abuse of the opiate OxyContin, which has resulted in numerous deaths, physicians facing criminal charges, and addicts attacking pharmacies. OxyContin is a legally prescribed substance, with appropriate medical uses—that is, it satisfies those conditions legalizers envision for cocaine and heroin. The point is clear: The laws are not the problem.

Former Sen. Daniel Patrick Moynihan observed that drugs place us in a dilemma: "We are required to choose between a crime problem and a public heath problem." Legalization is a dangerous mirage. To address a crime problem, we are asked to accept a public health crisis. Yet if we were to surrender, we would surely face both problems—intensified.

*"Prevention's social value is realized
through reductions in tobacco use, . . . in
decreased alcohol abuse . . . [and]
reductions in cocaine use."*

Drug Education Programs Can Reduce Drug Abuse

Drug Policy Research Center

The Drug Policy Research Center (DPRC), a division of
RAND, a nonprofit think tank, conducts research into and
provides analysis of drug-policy problems. In the following
viewpoint the DPRC discusses a new study on school-based
drug education programs showing that drug-prevention
programs can reduce teen use of alcohol, tobacco, and illicit
drugs. In addition, these drug-prevention programs are cost-
effective. While drug-prevention programs reduce lifetime
consumption of illicit and licit drugs by very small percentages, the savings to society are still high because the costs of
drug use are so high.

As you read, consider the following questions:
1. What are the tangible, measurable benefits used by the
   authors of the study to determine whether drug-
   prevention programs were cost-effective, as cited by the
   authors?
2. What are the program costs per participating student
   compared to society's quantifiable benefits, according to
   the study's authors?
3. What is the dominant cost of running drug-prevention
   programs, as cited by the authors?

The purpose of school-based drug prevention programs is to prevent, or at least diminish, children's use of a variety of substances, including licit substances such as alcohol and tobacco as well as illicit ones such as cocaine and marijuana. In fact, most successful school-based drug prevention programs, such as Lifeskills and Project ALERT, are not targeted to specific substances. Which drugs then, in terms of usage, do they affect? Where are the benefits of a drug prevention program realized? Through a reduction in crime related to a contracting cocaine market? Through higher productivity associated with diminished alcohol use? Or through less money spent on health care for smokers? To put the question more provocatively, are school-based drug prevention programs better viewed as a weapon in the war against illegal drug use or as a public health program for decreasing the adverse effects of licit substances?

The answers to such questions should provide a clearer understanding of the merits of a drug prevention program and limit unrealistic expectations of what such a program can accomplish. The answers to these questions also bear on funding sources for drug prevention and the types of programs drug prevention should be competing against for scarce resources. In a (2002) study, Drug Policy Research Center analysts Jonathan Caulkins, Rosalie Liccardo Pacula, Susan Paddock, and James Chiesa determined where drug prevention's benefits fall in terms of reductions in illicit-drug use, drinking, and smoking. They also evaluated whether the benefits of school-based drug prevention programs, in terms of reductions in the use of four substances—cocaine, marijuana, tobacco, and alcohol—exceed the costs of running the programs.

The DPRC estimates are limited to tangible, measurable benefits; they include reduced productivity losses and reductions in costs to government and the health care system, but not decreases in pain and suffering or decreased loss of life. The estimates apply to a hypothetical drug prevention program that is representative of successful real-world programs. The researchers did not seek to evaluate and contrast the relative merits of specific programs.

To first resolve the broad issue—whether the benefits of

a model school-based drug prevention program exceed its costs—Caulkins and his colleagues concluded that they apparently do. According to the researchers' best estimate (see Figure 1), society would currently realize quantifiable benefits of $840 from an average student's participation in drug prevention, compared with a program cost of $150 per participating student. The benefit estimate is subject to a number of assumptions, all of which are uncertain to some degree. The researchers repeatedly varied their assumptions to generate a large set of possible total benefit measures. About 95 percent of the time, the benefits exceeded $300, or twice the costs.

Figure 1. Benefits of School-Based Drug Prevention Are Probably Several Times Greater than the Costs

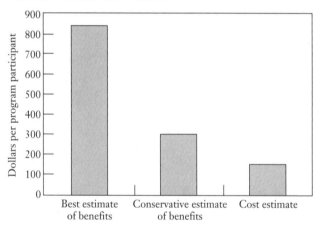

Both the best and the most conservative benefit estimates account for prevention's effects on only four substances—cocaine, marijuana, tobacco, and alcohol. These are the four drugs for which there is a sizable literature documenting prevention's effectiveness.

How are prevention's benefits apportioned across the four substances? Close to 40 percent of prevention's social value is realized through reductions in tobacco use, and more than a quarter of the value is in decreased alcohol abuse. Most of the remaining third of the value is associated with reductions in cocaine use; reductions in marijuana use account for a very small fraction of the total.

The DPRC researchers attempted to take into account other illegal drugs by assuming that drug prevention reduces the use of those drugs by as much as it reduces cocaine use. In that event, alcohol and tobacco would still account for two-thirds of the quantifiable social benefits from drug prevention. (See Figure 2.) It therefore makes more sense to view drug prevention principally as a public-health program rather than principally as a criminal justice intervention in the war on illicit drugs.

Figure 2. Most Benefits from School-Based Drug Prevention Are in the Form of Reductions in the Use of Legal Substances

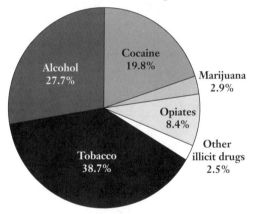

Implications for Funding

What do these findings imply about funding of school-based drug prevention? First, they suggest that model drug use prevention programs can be justified on a benefit-cost basis by the reductions in substance use. Drug prevention thus appears to be a wise use of the funds devoted to it. Whether it is the wisest use of those funds depends on whether there are other uses that could reap even greater social benefits.

If prevention should be viewed as a public health intervention, and not a criminal justice intervention, the implication might then be that school-based drug prevention should be funded out of health dollars rather than criminal justice dollars (or education dollars). At a minimum, if law enforcement interventions are seen as a higher priority for scarce justice program dollars, it would be foolish not to fund prevention if public health resources were available.

Issues of budgetary support should not obscure the fact that the dominant costs of running prevention programs are not dollar costs—e.g., for purchasing program materials. Rather, the dominant cost is from the lost learning opportunity on the part of students, the result of diverting scarce class time from traditional academic subjects to drug prevention education. Unless the school year is lengthened to compensate for the time diverted to drug prevention programs, the principal social cost of prevention will be the displacement of the time that would have been spent on instruction in traditional subjects.

An implication of this observation is that evaluators of future prevention programs might consider assessing the programs' effects on traditional educational objectives (in addition to and distinct from their impact on children's knowledge about drugs). If a drug prevention program were to include instruction in writing, exercises in critical thinking, or other such activities, as well as instruction in the school subjects it displaces, then its true economic cost would be less than $150 per participating student.

Scope of Effect: Small but Nevertheless Valuable

While cutting-edge prevention programs are a wise use of public funds, it is mainly because they are relatively cheap and because drug use is so costly to society, and not because the programs, even the model ones, eliminate a large proportion of drug use. In fact, the best estimates obtained by Caulkins and his colleagues are that prevention reduces lifetime consumption of tobacco by 2.3 percent, abuse of alcohol by 2.2 percent, and use of cocaine by 3.0 percent. Yet, even such small reductions in use can be very valuable because the social costs of drug use are so high. However, most of the reductions in use occur many years after the program is run, so the present value of those reductions, discounted at 4 percent per year, is only about half as great as their nominal value.

The estimated reductions in lifetime use may appear to be especially small given that the best prevention programs report reducing specific measures of use by 10 percent, 20 percent, or even as much as 30 percent. There are two principal reasons for this order-of-magnitude contrast:

First, programs are evaluated on many outcome measures. A single program's evaluation may find a 33 percent reduction in weekly use of a substance but only a 5 percent reduction in the probability of someone ever using the substance. The DPRC study's estimates are based on a program's effects using a consistent set of measures specified in advance, not measures selected ex post facto for which the impact was largest.

Second, prevention's effects usually decay over time. Effects on lifetime use are typically estimated to be only about 15 percent as great as the effects on use observed shortly after completion of an intervention.

School-based drug prevention is therefore a cost-effective tool for improving public health and for making incremental progress in the effort to manage mature drug epidemics, such as the U.S. cocaine epidemic. Furthermore, the study does not rule out the possibility that drug prevention programs may have an even greater impact on newly emerging epidemics than they have on the cocaine epidemic.

"*The most widely used drug-education program in America has never proven that it can prevent young people from using drugs.*"

Drug Education Programs Are Ineffective

Ryan H. Sager

In the following viewpoint Ryan H. Sager argues that studies of drug education programs such as Drug Abuse Resistance Education (DARE) have not shown any lasting effects in keeping children off drugs. While the program may influence children's views of drugs and drug use in the short term, the lessons are soon forgotten, he asserts. In the long term, there is little difference in rates of drug use between groups of students who have participated in DARE and those who have not. Sager contends that parents, schools, and society must discover a new way to talk to children about drugs. Sager is a freelance writer based in Washington, D.C.

As you read, consider the following questions:
1. What percent of students have tried illicit drugs by age eighteen, according to Sager?
2. What was the complaint DARE officials had about the study performed by researchers at the University of Kentucky, as cited by the author?
3. Why is Joel Brown skeptical of the DARE program, according to author?

Ryan H. Sager, "Teach Them Well: Drug Talk That Fails," *National Review*, vol. 52, May 1, 2000. Copyright © 2000 by National Review, Inc., 215 Lexington Ave., New York, NY 10016. Reproduced by permission.

Visit a college party, and you're likely to see people smoking cigarettes, drinking alcohol—and, quite often, smoking pot and using various other drugs. This scene will horrify some, but it won't surprise anyone familiar with to-day's college-age youth. Even though the generation of students now in college is the first to have been exposed to anti-drug messages since birth, a large portion of them seem not to have been convinced. By age 18, about 55 percent of students have tried some illicit drug, and 26 percent of college-age kids report having used an illicit drug within the last month. These numbers are up significantly from the beginning of the 1990s. This drug use may or may not represent a serious problem—most of these people go on to lead decent, productive lives—but it does testify to the ineffectiveness of anti-drug education and advertising in this country.

An Expensive Placebo

At a time when educators and the federal government are as committed as ever to the public-private Drug Abuse Resistance Education (DARE) program, and to a new $1-billion five-year taxpayer-funded anti-drug advertising campaign, it is appropriate to evaluate the return we're getting on this investment. If you ask anti-drug activists, some will say these programs have had a demonstrable impact on young people's attitudes toward drugs as well as their use of drugs. Others, however, are concerned that these programs have not proven their worth and could be diverting resources from more effective ways of preventing drug use by young people. According to this view, the public-education front of the drug war has been little more than an expensive placebo.

DARE, which costs approximately $220 million a year (including $1.75 million in taxpayer funding), is by far the most popular anti-drug program in American schools. About 75 percent of school districts use it. While parents and politicians tend to view DARE as sacred, most people are unaware that the program has long faced intense skepticism from experts. Although some studies have found positive effects (mostly attitude changes) over the short term, DARE has never been proven to have any lasting effect on the likeliness of children to use drugs later in life. Numerous studies, in fact, have found that the program has no long-term effect whatsoever. Sending police officers into classrooms to lecture children on the dangers of drugs—the gist of DARE's approach—may lower their opinions of drugs temporarily, but the lessons seem to fade quickly.

For years, DARE officials confronted with these negative studies have dismissed the studies as inadequate in scope. But a . . . study by researchers at the University of Kentucky should put those objections to rest. The study examined a group of young people ten years after they completed the DARE curriculum—and concluded that these students were just as likely to use drugs as a group of students who had been exposed to just a minimal drug-education curriculum in their health classes. Though DARE officials have complained that the study should have compared DARE students to students who had received no drug education at all, such a sample would be nearly impossible to find. Furthermore, the argument that DARE should be preserved even if it is no more effective than a shorter and less expensive program seems untenable.

Charlie Parsons, executive director of DARE America, doesn't believe the University of Kentucky study. He claims the program's curriculum has changed significantly since the period when the tracked students had it, and he puts his own spin on the data: "The effects dissipate somewhat, and that's not a surprise. It shows there's a need for reinforcement, and we totally agree with that." He even offers a solution to any problem that may exist: Extend the DARE program. The students in the University of Kentucky study were exposed to DARE only in elementary school. Mr. Parsons points to a study from Ohio University that shows lower drug use among students who continue with DARE during middle school and high school.

Skepticism

Despite Parsons's optimism, some researchers remain skeptical. Joel Brown, executive director of the Center for Educational Research and Development in Berkeley, questions the validity of the Ohio study on methodological grounds. He also notes that there is still no research showing that the program has any lasting effect.

More generally, Brown is skeptical of the "no-use" approach used by DARE and other programs. "The reality is that most kids will experiment with drugs," he says. He doesn't condone experimentation, but thinks a wiser approach would be "telling kids the truth about drugs trusting young people's ability to make decisions if given information." Brown thinks that kids who are at risk, or who already have problems with drugs, are unable to get useful advice from a program like DARE and could end up in deep trouble. Furthermore, Brown fears that when young people experiment with drugs (or observe others doing so) and find that the dire warnings they heard in DARE were overblown, they will feel that their elders have been lying to them for years. This, he says, could create "cognitive dissonance" that will lead them to reject not just the message but the messenger.

DEBATING CONTINUED USE OF THE DARE PROGRAM

Kirk. © 2001 by Kirk Anderson. Reproduced by permission.

The new anti-drug advertising campaign has the same problem: It has little room for a balanced view of drugs and is, for the most part, a variation on the theme of "Just say no." "It's just trying to scare people into not using drugs," says Brown. "There's no evidence that it really has an impact."

Impossible to Compare Programs

Whether or not it has an impact, of course, is an important question, now that the federal government has embarked on a $1-billion ad campaign. But it is almost impossible to study the effects of such a nationwide campaign on kids, because there is no control group—no similar kids who have not seen the ads—to use for comparison.

The Partnership for a Drug-Free America, the organization responsible for most of the anti-drug advertising on television, admits as much. Steve Dnistrian, a Partnership official, points to a correlation between anti-drug advertising and teenage drug use that he believes proves the effectiveness of the new ad campaign. "We're about two years into a very encouraging flattening, if not decline" in teenage drug use, he claims. In fact, according to the University of Michigan's annual Monitoring the Future study, from 1998 to 1999—the study's first opportunity to measure the effect of the new anti-drug ads—teen drug use actually increased (though to a lesser extent than in most years during the 1990s). More important, the flattening to which Dnistrian refers clearly predates the advertising campaign.

A Bleak Picture

What is left after a careful examination of anti-drug education and advertising is a fairly bleak picture for the anti-drug forces. The most widely used drug-education program in America has never proven that it can prevent young people from using drugs, and evidence for the effectiveness of anti-drug advertising is circumstantial at best. Hundreds of millions of dollars go into these programs every year, yet no one can point to any concrete results.

The problem is an anti-drug establishment with no interest in reconsidering its message, or even how the message is delivered. Kids know that smoking one joint will not ruin their lives, so telling them that it will can only make them more cynical than they already are. What we need is a fundamental rethinking of how we talk to kids about drugs. The government is not likely to do this anytime soon—so in the short term, it will be up to parents, alone, to give their kids realistic advice on drugs.

"More recovered alcoholics . . . began stable abstinence while attending Alcoholics Anonymous than while attending alcohol treatment centers."

Twelve-Step Treatment Programs Can Reduce Drug Abuse

Gene Hawes and Anderson Hawes

Gene Hawes, author of many books on alcoholism and addiction, and Anderson Hawes, a licensed professional clinical counselor and social worker, are the authors of *Addiction-Free: How to Help an Alcoholic or Addict Get Started on Recovery*, from which this viewpoint is excerpted. Alcoholics Anonymous (and similar programs for drug addicts) helps its alcoholic and drug-addicted members overcome their addictions by following a prescribed set of twelve steps. Longtime program members are also available to help counsel new members on how to get and stay clean and sober. The authors assert that these twelve-step programs have helped millions of people overcome their addictions to alcohol and drugs. In addition, studies of the programs have found that they are very successful in helping members kick their habits.

As you read, consider the following questions:
1. What is the difference between "open" and "closed" meetings, according to Hawes and Hawes?
2. What is the only requirement for membership in twelve-step programs, as cited by the authors?

Alcoholics Anonymous—widely termed simply AA—is the most widely available means for helping someone to recover from alcoholism/addiction. It is also very economical—it costs nothing. You'll find in AA people who know a great deal about addiction and how to get (and stay) clean and sober. These are also people who stand ready to help others start recovery and stay in it.

How AA Can Help

Each year, many thousands of women and men who have become addicted to alcohol and drugs start in recovery through AA. They're in all parts of the United States, and in many foreign countries. Those continuing in recovery as AA members now number some two million, according to AA reports at the time of this writing (May 2000).

(Statistics about AA are approximate and estimated. That they are approximations should be unimportant to you. The main point is this: Since AA helps millions of alcoholics/addicts start and stay in recovery, there's a good chance it may likewise help the person who is worrying you.). . .

Go to "Open" AA Meetings

When you're inquiring or being told about AA meetings nearby, you might ask especially about "Open" Meetings. Open Meetings are ones that nonalcoholics are permitted to attend. Most AA meetings are "closed" ones—for alcoholics/addicts only. Closed meetings are held mainly to protect the anonymity of members. Membership requirements are uniquely simple, and the individual—not AA—decides whether or not the individual is a member. AA's third "tradition" (a kind of constitutional provision) states: "The only requirement for membership is a desire to stop drinking."

Notice that being a member calls merely for "a desire" to stop drinking. Some who come in find that they can't stop drinking or drugging even though they want to do so. In many cases, though, members like these eventually do stop if they keep trying to get sober and keep going to AA meetings. . . .

Most (though not all) AA meetings are held in the early evenings, starting right after dinnertime at an hour like 7:00,

8:00, or 8:30. Meetings typically last one hour. Such timing is common for several vital reasons. That time of day is when many alcoholics/addicts most often started drinking or drugging. It comes after the day's work. It gives the recoverer a tremendously important goal that many feel (and find) they can attain: Don't have a drink or a drug just that day—hold on until the meeting tonight. However, a great many AA meetings are also held at all hours throughout the day, particularly in larger urban areas. . . .

The Addict Is Eligible

One objection the addict may raise is that her or his problem isn't alcohol—it's drugs. And after all, isn't this outfit *Alcoholics* Anonymous?

In reply, inform your addict that many AA groups today welcome persons with all varieties of substance-addiction problems. This is particularly true of AA groups in cities. Most recovering drug addicts today also abused alcohol as well as different drugs. Some rare AA members today abused only marijuana, or only crack cocaine, or only prescription drugs. But these new members are often welcomed all the same by their AA groups.

If your addict should encounter an AA group that seems a bit unfriendly, he or she could find and join another group whose members include some successfully recovering drug addicts. Many groups share a view commonly expressed at AA meetings: "A drug is a drug"—whether it's alcohol or cocaine, heroin or marijuana, Percodan or Valium, or whatever. Moreover, by basic principle, no AA group can exclude anyone who wants to join and states that he or she "has a desire to stop drinking"—AA's only membership requirement.

Narcotics Anonymous (NA) and Cocaine Anonymous (CA)

Two organizations similar to AA were organized for drug addicts in past years. One of these may appeal to your drug addict instead of AA. Narcotics Anonymous, or NA, and Cocaine Anonymous, or CA. NA and CA came into existence when a number of addicts found that AA's method and principles seemed to prove about as effective for drug addiction as for alcoholism. However, in those years several decades ago, many AA leaders and groups resisted opening AA to persons who were mainly drug addicts. These leaders feared that AA's proven value against alcoholism might be fatally compromised if AA should lose credibility by trying to counter drug addiction and failing. Some were concerned about the illegality of drugs.

Curiously, then, as a result, NA and CA were organized with exactly the same approach as AA. Even the same AA words were used for the basic "12 Steps" of NA and CA, with only the words *narcotics* and *cocaine* substituted for *alcohol.*

Compared to the number of AA groups, fewer NA and CA groups function today. Some NA or CA members prefer them to AA groups, feeling that the struggles of fellow addicts most closely parallel their own experience and thus better help bolster their recovery. . . .

Outside Experts Evaluate AA

You may be wondering what respected authorities independent of AA conclude about the program's effectiveness. Here are two examples.

Dr. Allen Frances and Dr. Michael B. First, who were respectively the task-force chairman and the editor of *DSM-IV*—the most recent edition of the definitive professional reference work for psychiatrists—say this about AA in their "layman's guide to the psychiatrist's bible," *Your Mental Health:*

> Alcoholics Anonymous (and its offshoots) is the great success story in the treatment of addictions. On any given day, more people go to AA groups around the world than attend any other form of therapy. The message of AA is compelling and translates very well across different drugs, social classes, and cultures. AA groups are so numerous and so varied that almost anyone can find a congenial one that is readily available, conveniently located, and probably meeting that night. AA provides hope, a philosophy of life, a spiritual reawakening, an emotional experience, concrete support, a sounding board, great advice, and help for family members. It is all the more remarkable that it does all this with virtually no bureaucracy or budget.

A second opinion on the value of AA is expressed by another psychiatrist, Dr. George E. Vaillant. Dr. Vaillant led and wrote a report on one of the most authoritative studies ever made of alcoholism and alcoholics. This monumental research project followed and analyzed the lives of more than six hundred persons for more than forty years. Its findings were presented in Dr. Vaillant's books, *The Natural History of Alcoholism* (1983) and *The Natural History of Alcoholism Revisited* (1995). In his second book, Dr. Vaillant stated:

> More recovered alcoholics from both groups [two large groups of men studied in the research] began stable abstinence while attending Alcoholics Anonymous than while attending alcohol treatment centers.

Dr. Vaillant added that, on the basis of findings for these two groups and an additional one he had studied:

> The numbers of subjects in these studies are small, and these results, drawn primarily from middle-aged white males, must be interpreted with caution. The implication from the three samples, however, is that a great many severely alcohol-dependent Americans, regardless of their social or psychological makeup, find help for their alcoholism through Alcoholics Anonymous.

Personal Histories

From the start, AA has relied on tremendously moving first-hand stories of individual men and women—who tell about their lives in the hope of getting other alcoholics/addicts started on recovery—rather than on statistics or research findings. As a speaker at an Open AA Meeting once put it when sharing what worked with him and what also works for others in his own twelve-step efforts: "When I say what I think, it has no power. But when I tell about my life and all that I've gone through—that has the power."

That power was one of AA's original startling discoveries. An alcoholic who is in fact recovering from alcoholism in many cases has more power than anyone else to break through to what AA calls to this day, "the still-suffering alcoholic."

The first-edition *Alcoholics Anonymous* volume of 1939 states:

> Highly competent psychiatrists who have dealt with us [alcoholics] have found it sometimes impossible to persuade an alcoholic to discuss his situation without reserve. Strangely

Controlled Drinking

There is no good evidence supporting the effectiveness of controlled drinking for chronic alcoholics. Why should it be offered as an alternative to abstinence training? However, it is logically possible that a small number of people suffering from alcohol abuse or alcohol dependence (alcoholism) could choose moderation over abstinence and benefit.

But, self-selection of treatment is currently impossible for many important reasons:. . .

[One] problem is the patient's diminished capacity; his or her inability to fully understand the information presented, integrate it and determine its relevance to self. Diminished capacity is common in alcohol-abusing patients due to the neurochemical effects of alcohol, either in terms of brain damage and consequent neuropsychological deficits, depression, panic, polydrug use and more.

A patient with diminished capacity is not fully autonomous, and is incapable of providing a valid informed consent and a reasoned treatment self-selection.

Irving Maltzman, *Counselor*, December 2000.

---

enough, wives, parents, and intimate friends usually find us even more unapproachable than do the psychiatrist and the doctor.

But the ex-problem drinker who has found this solution [AA], *who is properly armed with facts about himself, can generally win the entire confidence of another alcoholic in a few hours. Until such an understanding is reached, little or nothing can be accomplished.* [Italics in the original.]

Life Stories at the Open Meetings

You can experience the power of life stories like these directly—in person—at the major type of AA's Open Meetings. These are informally called "speaker" meetings. At them, the frequent custom is to have from one to three speakers "tell their stories."

Time-honored advice for telling your story calls for a speaker to cover three main things:
- what it used to be like, while "active" (that is, actively drinking/drugging);
- what happened to get you into recovery and AA; and
- what it's been like in recovery.

A meeting chairperson or other meeting leader introducing the speakers is very likely to set forth two vital guidelines for the listeners. One centers on AA's principle of anonymity. It is usually phrased, "What you hear here, and who you see here, let it stay here." Anything said, and anyone seen, are not to be mentioned to anyone outside that room.

Alcoholics/addicts attending are the target of the second admonition. "Identify. Don't compare," the leader typically warns. Identify with the feelings that a speaker sets forth, a leader often goes on to explain. Don't compare the disasters and troubles of a speaker with the disasters and troubles in your active-addiction days.

By comparing that you didn't have as many car wrecks or jailings or job losses or psych wards as a speaker did, you might compare yourself right out the door and back into drinking and drugging, the leader might add. But if you instead identify with a speaker's feelings, you'll know in your bones that you often felt (and sometimes still feel) exactly the same way.

If the alcoholic/addict you wish to help would be able to identify like this at Open Meetings, she or he might be strongly reinforced to get started in recovery. Especially if she or he should happen to have that electrifying experience of needing to gasp to a speaker: "You told *my* story!" Sooner or later, if the alcoholic/addict keeps attending meetings, just that happens. Always. . . .

Simplicity

Simplicity is a prime virtue of AA's program for surviving the ruinous and often fatal disease of alcoholism/addiction. Everything in AA aims at one supreme, single point: Don't drink or drug. Not in even the slightest quantity. Not for any reason, no matter what happens. Not at any moment.

In essence, this is the only fundamental element of AA that's absolutely necessary for recovery by the alcoholic/addict you're concerned about. Notoriously, though, one of the main definitions of an alcoholic/addict is someone who cannot possibly stop.

So, AA members ask the newcomer, can you stop just for one day—*this* day, now? The newcomer who doesn't need detox badly enough, and who is already hitting bottom badly enough, will say yes.

Fine, say AA members. We just don't drink or drug "one day at a time." *This* day. Today. And we get to an AA meeting tonight. Every night, at first.

At the meeting, members say, you'll find that we're all kinds of people who know all about how to stay away from a drink or a drug one day at a time. We will welcome you, and we'll offer to help you by really caring about you—the way others cared about us when we were new. You'll learn from us how we've gone through all that you've gone through. (Some of us have gone through even more.) You'll learn what we do so that we still don't have to drink or drug.

And, with us, they say, you'll find that you don't have to drink or drug today, either. If you do what we do, you'll get what we've got: a life, a life clean and sober, a good life, in recovery.

AA Members Help the Alcoholic/Addict

Passages earlier in the viewpoint told about AA's discovery of the unique power often possessed by a recovering alcoholic/addict to get an active alcoholic/addict started on recovery. AA made an even more important companion discovery concerning such power. This power works both ways—it works on the alcoholic/addict trying to help, as much as on the alcoholic/addict needing help. In fact, it typically proves more consistently effective on the helper than on the one being helped.

Discovery of this reverse effect on the helper marked the founding of AA. Future founder Bill W. discovered that he could not preserve his own then-new and shaky sobriety alone, by his own efforts. He could save his sobriety, his freedom from addiction, only by trying to help a hopelessly addicted and alcoholic Akron physician, Dr. Bob S., to start on recovery.

Bill did try (essentially by telling Dr. Bob his story), and stayed sober himself. The date of Dr. Bob's last drink, on June 10, 1935, is AA's founding date. Dr. Bob is the other founder. Each of the two drunks helping the other stayed sober. Alone, neither could do it.

"Passing It On"

Ever since then, every AA member gratefully recalls getting extraordinary help when new to the program from longer-experienced members who said that any all-out help they gave greatly protected their own sobriety. They were passing it on, giving to others what had been given to them.

Helping others to recover as the best protection of one's own recovery thus became one of the most effective parts of the "message" invented by AA—the message that here at last in human history is a way by which a great many previously hopeless alcoholics/addicts actually are recovering. AA members today accordingly try to "carry this message to alcoholics," as it says in AA's Twelfth Step.

"You Can't Do It Alone—and You Don't Have To"

In almost anything he or she does in AA, the alcoholic/addict you care about will be helped by members carrying the message to him or her with their actions and words. In turn, your alcoholic/addict is likely to start helping in simple ways, such as going to and honestly speaking up in meetings, talking with others before and after meetings, setting up and putting away meeting chairs, and phoning other men (for a man) or women (for a woman) who are members. Getting involved with others in ways like these has been found extremely important to promoting recovery.

"It's a *we* program," members often observe. "I drank and drugged alone, but we get sober together."

"You can't do this thing alone," one member recalls having been told in his early days. He was immensely heartened to hear what followed: "And you don't have to."

"The vast majority of people who overcome addictions . . . do so without treatment and without participation in [Alcoholics Anonymous]."

Most Twelve-Step Treatment Programs Are Ineffective at Reducing Drug Abuse

James DeSena

Author James DeSena argues in the following viewpoint, excerpted from his book *Overcoming Your Alcohol, Drug, and Recovery Habits*, that the rosy pictures painted by twelve-step drug and alcohol treatment programs such as Alcoholics Anonymous (AA) are distorted. These treatment programs help very few addicts overcome their addiction, he contends, yet the twelve-step community insists that addicts who relapse go through the program again and again. DeSena contends that most people overcome their addictions on their own without going through any sort of treatment program.

As you read, consider the following questions:

1. How do twelve-step advocates interpret doubts expressed about the program, in DeSena's opinion?
2. What are the ranges of percentages of alcoholics who recovered on their own without treatment, as cited by the author?
3. Why should AA's figures for numbers of alcoholics who were successfully treated be questioned, in DeSena's opinion?

James DeSena, *Overcoming Your Alcohol, Drug, and Recovery Habits: An Empowering Alternative to AA and 12-Step Treatment*. Tucson, AZ: See Sharp Press, 2003.

The early morning quiet was shattered when Brynn Hartman, wife of actor Phil Hartman, shot Phil and then turned the gun on herself. She was recovering after drug and alcohol treatment. When [rock star] Curt Cobain pulled the trigger on the shotgun he jammed in his mouth, he was recovering after drug and alcohol treatment. When Terri McGovern, daughter of former U.S. Senator George McGovern, died of exposure in a snow bank, she was recovering after drug and alcohol treatment. When his cocaine-ravaged heart could take no more, 50-year-old former all star and World Series MVP Darrell Porter was found dead in a park; he was recovering after drug and alcohol treatment. When he blew his brains out, Hugh O'Connor, son of [actor] Carroll O'Connor, was recovering after drug and alcohol treatment. When years of substance abuse finally killed [rock star] Jerry Garcia, he was receiving, yet again, drug and alcohol treatment. When [rock star] Andy Gibb drank and drugged himself to death, he was recovering after drug and alcohol treatment. When [comic] Chris Farley drank and drugged himself to death, he too was recovering.

All are gone. Addictions kill—so it seems.

Trick or Treatment?

The best-kept secret of America's addiction treatment industry is that it tricks much more that it treats. While their public relations pitchmen paint rosy pictures as they showcase a few newly sober or high-profile celebrities, casualties such as those above, and countless others, continue to pile up. They are not simply victims of addictions. They are the sacrificial lambs of an addiction treatment industry (ATI) that boasts, "Treatment works!"

Addiction treatment initiates you into the precarious world of recovery—and recovery programs are everywhere. Booze, other drugs, gambling, food, sex, love, computers. If you can abuse it, there's a program to deal with it. The trouble begins when your abuse develops into addiction. That trouble is magnified when your addiction is labeled a disease. Confusion sets in when the "treatment" for your "disease" requires lifetime membership in quasi-religious societies disguised as recovery programs.

If this sounds strange to you, you're not alone. Such "treatment" benefits only a select few, a fact which has become very obvious. This religious "treatment" is no longer acceptable as the universal remedy for compulsive behavior and addiction. What benefits *you* is the point! You're better off without addictions *and* without "recovery." You can achieve freedom from both. Begin your liberation now by learning what went wrong—and how you can make it right.

The Sacred Cow

Recovery from compulsive behaviors and addictions has become synonymous with the 12-step program of Alcoholics Anonymous. Like aspirin, the steps are prescribed routinely. Worse, despite overwhelming research evidence to the contrary, 12-step programs are prescribed as the only things that work: "Take the steps and call your sponsor. If that doesn't help, you may change your sponsor, but you must take the steps because the steps are the only thing that works." But they don't work for everyone. Far from it. But that matters not at all to 12-step promoters, especially those in the addiction treatment industry.

Twelve-step advocates, especially AA members, interpret the slightest doubts about The Program as personal affronts and condemnation of their beliefs. Martin E.P. Seligman, Ph.D., Kogod Professor and Director of Clinical Training in Psychology at the University of Pennsylvania, confirms this in his book, *What You Can Change and What You Can't:*

> AA does not welcome scientific scrutiny . . . AA is a sacred cow. Criticism of it is rare, and testimonial praise is almost universal. The organization has been known to go after its most trenchant critics as if they were heretics, so criticism, even in the scientific literature, is timid.

A large majority of addiction therapists/counselors promote AA. Not surprisingly, most are AA members. They interpret their clients' "undisciplined" questioning of The Program as typical alcoholic behavior steeped in egotism, riotous self-will and, of course, denial. They are also extremely, reflexively defensive, labeling mere questioning of their methods or motives as "AA bashing." In sum, AA and, especially, its commercial branch, the addiction treatment industry, is an ineffective, self-absorbed, monolithic institution whose members work assiduously to deny addicted people life-saving information and alternative modes of recovery. Of course, many of those who do this have good intentions, but they do it nonetheless.

The Recovery Group Movement (RGM)

The recovery group movement drives America's addiction treatment industry. It's a collective effort of people promoting the "treatment works" mantra—authors, AA members, prominent "recovering" people, and, above all, those who own and work in the treatment industry. Under the guise of treatment, they advance their 12-step agenda as a cure-all. The major flaw with the RGM's one-size-fits-all "treatment" plan, is that it does not work, never has worked, and never will work. It is simply not the panacea the RGM touts it to be. Martin Seligman puts it well:

> AA is not for everyone. It is spiritual, even outright religious, and so repels the secular-minded. It demands group adherence, and so repels the nonconformist. It is confessional, and so repels those with a strong sense of privacy. Its goal is total abstinence, not a return to social drinking. It holds alcoholism to be a disease, not a vice or a frailty. One or more of these premises are unacceptable to many alcoholics, and these people will probably drop out.

> As for outpatient psychotherapy, *there is no evidence that any form of talking therapy—not psychoanalysis, not supportive therapy, not cognitive therapy—can get you to give up alcohol.* . . . Overall, recovery from alcohol abuse, unlike recovery from a compound fracture, does not depend centrally on what kind of inpatient or outpatient treatment you get, or whether you get any treatment at all. (Emphasis added)

Why do you think so many people bounce in and out of 12-step programs, or check into rehabs three, four, five times and more? The RGM's stock answers range from disease to denial to "grave mental and emotional disorders" (as AA literature states). Society must realize that these "diagnoses" were invented by AA and accepted as fact by a perverse addiction treatment industry largely made up of AA members. This AA make-believe causes needless suffering and death for countless people who innocently present themselves for addiction treatment.

201

Self-Recovery

What the recovery group movement won't tell you is that the vast majority of people who overcome addictions (that is, actually get over addictions, rather than remain stuck "in recovery" forever) do so without treatment and without participation in AA. Consider the following from the Harvard Medical School's *Mental Health Letter*, August/September 1996:

> *Most recovery from alcoholism is not the result of treatment.* Only 20% of alcohol abusers are ever treated. . . . Alcohol addicts, like heroin addicts, have a tendency to mature out of their addiction. . . .
>
> In [a] group of self-treated alcoholics, more than half said that they had simply thought it over and decided that alcohol was bad for them. A[nother group] said health problems and frightening experiences such as accidents and blackouts persuaded them to quit. . . . Others have recovered by changing their circumstances with the help of a new job or a new love or under the threat of a legal crisis or the breakup of a family. (Italics added)

And study results from highly respected addiction researchers, Doctors Linda and Mark Sobell, confirm Harvard's 20%-treatment statistic:

> [S]urveys found that over 77 percent of those who had overcome an alcohol problem had done so without treatment. In an earlier study . . . a sizable majority of alcohol abusers, 82 percent, recovered on their own.

Yet doctors, employers, ministers, family and friends automatically recommend 12-step programs as the road to recovery. Under the umbrella of addiction treatment our courts mandate addicted criminals to rehab/AA in lieu of prison. Addicted prison inmates are denied parole and/or privileges unless they attend AA. Employee assistance programs order AA participation under threat of job loss. Driving privileges remain revoked unless a convicted drunk driver attends AA. Professional licenses are suspended if addicted lawyers or doctors do not attend AA.

If you have any type of "addiction" problem, you must be in a 12-step program, they insist. But should you find The Program ineffective, or question it in any way, you're branded a dissenter, a malcontent in obvious denial who is playing God and is not serious about wanting recovery unless it's on your own ego-inflated terms. Should you relapse, it's back to square one—step 1.

So, what's the upshot of all this? If you have (or even have had) some type of addiction or abuse problem, the unequivocal conclusion of addiction specialists and the entire 12-step community is that there must be something terribly wrong with you. You are placed, or must place yourself, back into the recovery process again and again and again. Rarely is it suggested that The Program offered is simply not beneficial to you. Still more rare is information on the high incidence of self-recovery and the "secret" to accomplishing it.

AA and Criminals

A 1997 survey conducted at the University of Georgia found that more than 90 percent of private treatment programs are based on AA's 12 steps [which are part of AA's abstinence treatment program]. Why, then, is our prison population at record levels, and why is so much of this crime associated with substance abuse? [Oklahoma governor Frank] Keating approvingly refers to a Department of Justice finding that most criminals are substance abusers, including a "staggering 83 percent of state inmates." Keating cites several studies that have found that inmates who complete treatment and continue to attend AA have better records than untreated prisoners and parolees. However, studies that include dropouts from treatment groups in their calculations have reported different results. For instance, a 1999 study of Texas' correctional substance abuse treatment programs found that those who participated in an in-prison program had the same recidivism rates as non-participants. Although those who completed the program did better than untreated offenders, those who entered but did not complete the program did worse. Moreover, probationers enrolled in treatment in Texas had an overall higher recidivism rate than non-participants.

Stanton Peele, *Reason*, May 2001.

Instead, you are found guilty of not responding to a spiritual program that is wrongly yet reverently viewed as the cure-all for every addiction. While the old saying, "If at first you don't succeed try, try again" is viable in some circumstances, there comes a time for reflection—a time to stop beating a dead horse and realistically question and reevaluate your methods and motives.

Your life might depend on it. While it's too late to ask Chris, Jerry, Curt, Andy, Hugh, Brynn, Darrell, Phil, or Terri, it's not too late for you. So run—run away as far as possible and as fast as you can from *anyone* who tells you that Alcoholics Anonymous and its 12-step program is the only road to recovery or the best way to recover.

Just Ask Joan

Jumping in and out of 12-step programs, enduring multiple rehab stints, months of addiction counseling, therapy, relapse prevention, and aftercare programs, along with meetings on top of meetings, are all part of a phenomenon I have termed the *recovery merry-go-round*. Only it's not merry and it's often more exasperating than the roller coaster of addiction. The reality is that people caught in the downward spiral of addictive behavior are not recovering, no matter how many times they go through a misguided treatment process, which ritually incorporates a 12-step agenda. Just ask Joan Kennedy [former wife of Senator Ted Kennedy]—if you can catch her in-between rehab treatments (13 by last count).

It's clear: 12-step based treatment and recovery programs are not the universal answer to overcoming addiction. Yet, time after time people like Mrs. Kennedy are recycled through a twisted process that fails much more than it succeeds. Besides the Mrs. Kennedys, of the 20% who are "treated," it's the Chris Farleys, Brynn Hartmans, and Curt Cobains that we constantly hear about. Even counselors and therapists who are not ardent 12-step supporters jump on the ATI bandwagon, and will "treat" you, for years on end, with the latest in recovery psychobabble. This is the insanity of the recovery group movement and the addiction treatment industry. And it is only a portion of the devastation wrought by the recovery merry-go-round. . . .

Success Rates

What constitutes success in AA's recovery program? In the foreword to the second edition of the Big Book they write:

> Of alcoholics who came to AA and really tried, 50% got sober at once and remained that way, 25% sobered up after

some relapses, and among the remainder, those who stayed on with AA showed improvement.

In Appendix III, "The Medical View on AA," Dr. G. Kirby Collier, Psychiatrist writes:

> Any therapeutic or philosophic procedure which can prove a recovery rate of 50% to 60% must merit our consideration.

First, please note that these figures are pure assertion. The Big Book offers no evidence whatsoever in support of them. Second, please note that the Big Book carefully qualifies AA's alleged success rate by counting only those who "really tried." And even if you accept these self-serving, unsupported figures, this still means that 25% to 50% of those who "really try" do not achieve success through AA. Should these AA "failures" be conveniently categorized as "in denial," hopeless or unwilling to change?

The Big Book's alleged "success" percentages are over 60 years old and reflect an AA membership that actively sought out The Program. Those figures may have been accurate when enrollment numbered a few dozen, but they are not relevant today. And dropout rates are never mentioned. Instead, AA deals only with those who "really tried."

The only two controlled studies of AA ever conducted both concluded that AA's success rate is no better than the rate of spontaneous remission; that is, those who participated in AA did no better than those who were left totally on their own. Despite that, the RGM boasts of AA's "unparalleled success" based on uncontrolled studies. But AA's own most recent surveys reveal huge dropout rates: 75% after ten meetings, and 95% before one year. Of the 5% who last a year, only 45% reach at least five years sobriety. This means that fewer than three in 100 people entering AA achieve five years sobriety. If AA claims a 3% success rate from its own surveys, it must also take responsibility for its dismal 97% failure rate.

It's also worth noting that the 3% success rate does not refer to those who have stayed continuously booze free. Rather, it refers to continuous membership in AA, which is most definitely not the same thing as continuous abstinence. To paraphrase Ken Ragge (author of *The Real AA*), the only thing more common in AA than abstinence is binge drinking. Because of this, 12-step treatment providers and other AA members regard relapse as a normal part of the "recovery process." And, incredibly, Alcoholics Anonymous is still touted by the RGM as the only thing that works! The sad fact is that AA works very well—for very few.

What about people ordered to attend AA, who would otherwise not be there? Consider the following from the Harvard Medical School's *Mental Health Letter:*

> Since assignments to AA are sometimes made by courts, probation officials, and parole boards, a form of controlled research is possible. One study found no long-term difference between problem drinkers assigned at random by a court to Alcoholics Anonymous and a control group assigned to no treatment. Another investigation compared alcoholic heroin addicts who were given methadone alone with addicts assigned to AA and members of another group trained in controlled drinking. Among the patients who completed treatment (fewer than 20%), AA was least effective.

Periodical Bibliography

The following articles have been selected to supplement the diverse views presented in this chapter.

William J. Bennett	"Don't Surrender," *Wall Street Journal*, May 15, 2001.
Brian Bergman	"Just Say 'Yes': Legalizing Marijuana Would Actually Be Safer for Kids than Decriminalization," *Maclean's*, March 3, 2003.
Fox Butterfield	"New Drug-Offender Program Draws Unexpected Clients," *New York Times*, September 29, 2001.
Joseph A. Califano Jr.	"A Turning Point on Drugs," *Washington Post*, March 13, 2001.
Clifton Coles	"Alternatives to Growing Drugs: First World Policies That Keep Food Cheap Counteract the War on Drugs," *Futurist*, May/June 2003.
Thomas G. Donlon	"Unintended Consequences: The War on Drugs Is a Self-Punishing Mistake," *Barron's*, June 24, 2002.
Steven Duke	"End the Drug War," *Social Research*, Fall 2001.
Economist	"Breaking Convention: Illicit Drugs," April 5, 2003.
John Gould	"Zone Defense: Drug-Free School Zones Were Supposed to Keep Dealers Away from Kids," *Washington Monthly*, June 2002.
Christopher Lord	"The Poppies That Feed the Farmers," *New Statesman*, April 22, 2002.
Ken MacQueen	"Getting Addicts off the Streets," *Maclean's*, March 17, 2003.
David Masci	"Preventing Teen Drug Use: Is the 'Get-Tough' Approach Effective?" *CQ Researcher*, March 15, 2002.
Ed Sanow	"Old Problem, New DARE," *Law and Order*, April 2001.
Peter Schrag	"A Quagmire for Our Time," *American Prospect*, August 13, 2001.
Joan Kennedy Taylor	"Ending the War on Drugs," *Free Inquiry*, Spring 2002.
Sanho Tree	"'They Do It Because They Make Money,'" *Sojourners*, May/June 2003.
Charles Van Deventer	"I'm Proof: The War on Drugs Is Working," *Newsweek*, July 2, 2001.

For Further Discussion

Chapter 1

1. John P. Walters points to an incident where gangs of marijuana dealers killed more than two dozen people in the course of doing business over several years in the District of Columbia to help support his argument that marijuana is a dangerous drug. Do you agree that this street violence makes marijuana a dangerous drug that should remain illegal? Why or why not?

2. Jon Cole, Harry Sumnall, and Charles Grob assert that studies showing that drugs such as Ecstasy are not as harmful as believed are not published, or, he claims, results are ignored by researchers and scientific journals. The authors contend that misrepresentation of the data has had fatal consequences; therefore, they argue that accurate information, both negative and positive, should be provided. Do you agree? Why or why not?

3. Steroids are extremely effective in building muscle mass, increasing endurance, and reducing fat, yet they also have well-known and documented adverse side effects, such as inducing irritability and aggression, reducing sperm production, and, in women, encouraging the growth of excessive body hair. Other risks include increased dangers of heart attacks, strokes, and liver cancer. Review the viewpoints on steroids in this chapter and list other side effects associated with their use. In your opinion, do the benefits of steroid use outweigh the risks? Explain your answer.

Chapter 2

1. Alan I. Leshner concedes that addiction begins as a choice made by the user, but he argues that drug use fundamentally changes the brain, which is why addicts are unable to quit. Jeffrey A. Schaler contends that addiction is not a disease because only the results of addiction—and not addiction itself—are visible in the body. Whose argument do you find more convincing and why?

2. Many authors in this book argue over the gateway theory—whether using marijuana leads to the use of harder drugs such as cocaine and heroin. Based on your readings of the viewpoints, do you believe marijuana is a gateway drug? Support your answer with examples from the viewpoints.

3. After reading the viewpoints in this chapter, which factors do you believe play the greatest role in determining drug abuse? Explain your answer.

Chapter 3

1. The U.S. Supreme Court has ruled that testing students who participate in extracurricular activities for drug use is constitutional but testing pregnant women for drug use is unconstitutional. What are the main differences in these two types of cases? Do you agree with the Court's decisions? Why or why not?

2. OHS Health and Safety Services, Inc., maintains that drug use in the workplace is a serious problem, and supports employee drug testing. OHS is a business that initiates and administers drug-free workplace programs for large and small companies. Does knowing what OHS does influence your assessment of its argument? Explain.

Chapter 4

1. John P. Walters and Gary E. Johnson disagree on whether legalization is the way to solve America's drug problems. Based on your reading of the viewpoints, do you think legalizing some—or all—illicit drugs would reduce or increase America's drug problems? Explain.

2. Both Ryan H. Sager and the Drug Policy Research Center (DPRC) agree that the effectiveness of drug education programs such as DARE decline over time. However, DPRC contends that DARE programs are still worthwhile because they have been shown to decrease alcohol and tobacco use among teens. In your opinion, do the benefits gained by drug education classes justify the time lost that could be spent studying more traditional academic subjects? Why or why not?

Organizations to Contact

The editors have compiled the following list of organizations concerned with the issues debated in this book. The descriptions are derived from materials provided by the organizations. All have publications or information available for interested readers. The list was compiled on the date of publication of the present volume; the information provided here may change. Be aware that many organizations take several weeks or longer to respond to inquiries, so allow as much time as possible.

American Civil Liberties Union (ACLU)
125 Broad St., 18th Fl., New York, NY 10004-2400
(212) 549-2500
e-mail: aclu@aclu.org • website: www.aclu.org

The ACLU is a national organization that works to defend Americans' civil rights guaranteed by the U.S. Constitution. It provides legal defense, research, and education. The ACLU opposes the criminal prohibition of marijuana and the civil liberties violations that result from it. Its publications include ACLU Briefing Paper #19: *Against Drug Prohibition* and *Ira Glasser on Marijuana Myths and Facts.*

American Council for Drug Education (ACDE)
164 W. Seventy-fourth St., New York, NY 10023
(800) 488-DRUG (3784) • (212) 595-5810, ext. 7860
fax: (212) 595-2553
website: www.acde.org

The American Council for Drug Education informs the public about the harmful effects of abusing drugs and alcohol. It gives the public access to scientifically based, compelling prevention programs and materials. ACDE has resources for parents, youth, educators, prevention professionals, employers, health care professionals, and other concerned community members who are working to help America's youth avoid the dangers of drug and alcohol abuse.

Canadian Centre on Substance Abuse (CCSA)
75 Albert St., Suite 300, Ottawa, ON K1P 5E7 Canada
(613) 235-4048 • fax: (613) 235-8101
e-mail: admin@ccsa.ca • website: www.ccsa.ca

Established in 1988 by an Act of Parliament, CCSA works to minimize the harm associated with the use of alcohol, tobacco, and other drugs. It disseminates information on the nature, extent, and consequences of substance abuse; sponsors public debates on the topic; and supports organizations involved in substance abuse treatment, prevention, and educational programming. The centre publishes the newsletter *Action News* six times a year.

Canadian Foundation for Drug Policy (CFDP)

70 MacDonald St., Ottawa, ON K2P 1H6 Canada
(613) 236-1027 • fax: (613) 238-2891
e-mail: eoscapel@fox.nstn.ca
website: http://fox.nstn.ca/~eoscapel/cfdp/cfdp.html

Founded by several of Canada's leading drug policy specialists, CFDP examines the objectives and consequences of Canada's drug laws and policies, including laws prohibiting marijuana. When necessary, the foundation recommends alternatives that it believes would make Canada's drug policies more effective and humane. CFDP discusses drug policy issues with the Canadian government, media, and general public. It also disseminates educational materials and maintains a website.

Cato Institute

1000 Massachusetts Ave. NW, Washington, DC 20001-5403
(202) 842-0200
e-mail: cato@cato.org • website: www.cato.org

The institute is a public policy research foundation dedicated to limiting the control of government and to protecting individual liberty. Cato, which strongly favors drug legalization, publishes the *Cato Journal* three times a year and the *Cato Policy Report* bimonthly.

Committees of Correspondence

11 John St., Room 506, New York, NY 10038
(212) 233-7151 • fax: (212) 233-7063

The Committees of Correspondence is a national coalition of community groups that campaign against drug abuse among youth by publishing data about drugs and drug abuse. The coalition opposes drug legalization and advocates treatment for drug abusers. Its publications include the quarterly *Drug Abuse Newsletter*, the periodic *Drug Prevention Resource Manual*, and related pamphlets, brochures, and article reprints.

Drug Enforcement Administration (DEA)

Mailstop: AXS, 2401 Jefferson Davis Hwy., Alexandria, VA 22301
(202) 307-1000
website: www.usdoj.gov/dea

The DEA is the federal agency charged with enforcing the nation's drug laws. The agency concentrates on stopping the smuggling and distribution of narcotics in the United States and abroad. It publishes the *Drug Enforcement Magazine* three times a year.

Drug Policy Foundation
4455 Connecticut Ave. NW, Suite B-500
Washington, DC 20008-2328
(202) 537-5005 • fax: (202) 537-3007
e-mail: dpf@dpf.org • website: www.dpf.org

The foundation, an independent nonprofit organization, supports and publicizes alternatives to current U.S. policies on illegal drugs, including marijuana. The foundation's publications include the bimonthly *Drug Policy Letter* and the book *The Great Drug War*. It also distributes *Press Clips*, an annual compilation of newspaper articles on drug legalization issues, as well as legislative updates.

Family Research Council
801 G St. NW, Washington, DC 20001
(202) 393-2100 • order line: (800) 225-4008 • fax: (202) 393-2134
e-mail: corrdept@frc.org • website: www.frc.org

The council analyzes issues affecting the family and seeks to ensure that the interests of the traditional family are considered in the formulation of public policy. It lobbies legislatures and promotes public debate on issues concerning the family. The council publishes articles and position papers against the legalization of medicinal marijuana.

Heritage Foundation
214 Massachusetts Ave. NE, Washington, DC 20002-2302
(202) 546-4400

The Heritage Foundation is a conservative public policy research institute that opposes the legalization of drugs and advocates strengthening law enforcement to stop drug abuse. It publishes position papers on a broad range of topics, including drug issues. Its regular publications include the monthly *Policy Review*, the Backgrounder series of occasional papers, and the Heritage Lecture series.

Lindesmith Center
400 W. Fifty-ninth St., New York, NY 10019
(212) 548-0695 • fax: (212) 548-4670
e-mail: lindesmith@sorosny.org • website: www.lindesmith.org

The Lindesmith Center is a policy research institute that focuses on broadening the debate on drug policy and related issues. The center houses a library and information center; organizes seminars and conferences; acts as a link between scholars, government, and the media; directs a grant program in Europe; and undertakes projects on drug policy topics, including medicinal marijuana. It addresses issues of drug policy reform through a variety of projects, including the Drug Policy Seminar series, the International Harm Reduction Development Program, and the Methadone Policy Reform Project. The center's website includes articles, polls, and legal documents relating to marijuana.

Marijuana Policy Project
PO Box 77492-Capitol Hill, Washington, DC 20013
(202) 462-5747 • fax: (202) 232-0442
e-mail: mpp@mpp.org • website: www.mpp.org
The Marijuana Policy Project develops and promotes policies to minimize the harm associated with marijuana. It is the only organization that is solely concerned with lobbying to reform the marijuana laws on the federal level. The project increases public awareness through speaking engagements, educational seminars, the mass media, and briefing papers.

Media Awareness Project (MAP)
PO Box 651, Porterville, CA 93258
(800) 266-5759
e-mail: mgreer@mapinc.org • website: www.mapinc.org
MAP is an international network of activists dedicated to drug policy reform, with an emphasis on impacting public opinion and media coverage of drug policy issues. It opposes the criminal justice/prosecution/interdiction model of drug policy and favors a more liberal approach. MAP publishes the weekly *DrugSense* newsletter and makes tens of thousands of drug policy–related articles available on its website.

Multidisciplinary Association for Psychedelic Studies (MAPS)
2121 Commonwealth Ave., Suite 220, Charlotte, NC 28205
(704) 334-1798 • fax: (704) 334-1799
e-mail: info@maps.org • website: www.maps.org
MAPS is a membership-based research and educational organization. It focuses on the development of beneficial, socially sanctioned uses of psychedelic drugs and marijuana. MAPS helps scientific researchers obtain governmental approval for, fund, conduct, and report on psychedelic research in human volunteers. It publishes the quarterly *MAPS Bulletin* as well as various reports and newsletters.

National Center on Addiction and Substance Abuse (CASA)
Columbia University
152 W. Fifty-seventh St., New York, NY 10019-3310
(212) 841-5200 • fax: (212) 956-8020
website: www.casacolumbia.org

CASA is a private nonprofit organization that works to educate the public about the hazards of chemical dependency. The organization supports treatment as the best way to reduce chemical dependency. It produces publications describing the harmful effects of alcohol and drug addiction and effective ways to address the problem of substance abuse.

National Clearinghouse for Alcohol and Drug Information
PO Box 2345, Rockville, MD 20847-2345
(800) 729-6686 • (301) 468-2600 • fax: (301) 468-6433
e-mail: shs@health.org • website: www.health.org

The clearinghouse distributes publications of the U.S. Department of Health and Human Services, the National Institute on Drug Abuse, and other federal agencies concerned with alcohol and drug abuse. Brochure titles include *Tips for Teens About Marijuana.*

National Institute on Drug Abuse (NIDA)
U.S. Department of Health and Human Services
5600 Fishers Ln., Rockville, MD 20857
(301) 443-6245
e-mail: Information@lists.nida.nih • website: www.nida.nih.gov

NIDA supports and conducts research on drug abuse—including the yearly Monitoring the Future Survey—to improve addiction prevention, treatment, and policy efforts. It publishes the bimonthly *NIDA Notes* newsletter, the periodic NIDA Capsules fact sheets, and a catalog of research reports and public education materials, such as *Marijuana: Facts for Teens* and *Marijuana: Facts Parents Need to Know.*

National Organization for the Reform of Marijuana Laws (NORML)
1001 Connecticut Ave. NW, Suite 710, Washington, DC 20036
(202) 483-5500 • fax: (202) 483-0057
e-mail: natlnorml@aol.com • website: www.norml.org

NORML fights to legalize marijuana and to help those who have been convicted and sentenced for possessing or selling marijuana. In addition to pamphlets and position papers, it publishes the newsletter *Marijuana Highpoints*, the bimonthly *Legislative Bulletin* and *Freedom@NORML*, and the monthly *Potpourri.*

NORML Canada

14846 Jane St., King City, ON L7B 1A3 Canada
(905) 833-3167 • fax: (905) 833-3682
e-mail: iorfida@interlog.com • website: www.calyx.com/~normlca

NORML Canada believes the discouragement of marijuana through use of criminal law has been excessively costly and harmful to both society and individuals. Although it does not advocate or encourage the use of marijuana, NORML Canada works at all levels of government to eliminate criminal penalties for private marijuana use.

Office of National Drug Control Policy

Executive Office of the President
Drugs and Crime Clearinghouse
PO Box 6000, Rockville, MD 20849-6000
e-mail: ondcp@ncjrs.org
website: www.whitehousedrugpolicy.gov

The Office of National Drug Control Policy is responsible for formulating the government's national drug strategy and the president's antidrug policy as well as coordinating the federal agencies responsible for stopping drug trafficking. Drug policy studies are available upon request.

Partnership for a Drug-Free America

405 Lexington Ave., Suite 1601, New York, NY 10174
(212) 922-1560 • fax: (212) 922-1570
website: www.drugfreeamerica.org

The Partnership for a Drug-Free America is a nonprofit organization that utilizes media communication to reduce demand for illicit drugs in America. Best known for its national antidrug advertising campaign, the partnership works to "unsell" drugs to children and to prevent drug use among kids. It publishes the annual *Partnership Newsletter* as well as monthly press releases about current events with which the partnership is involved.

Bibliography of Books

Nikki Babbit — *Adolescent Drug and Alcohol Abuse: How to Spot It, Stop It, and Get Help for Your Family.* Sebastapol, CA: O'Reilly, 2000.

Rachel Green Baldino — *Welcome to Methadonia: A Social Worker's Candid Account of Life in a Methadone Clinic.* Harrisburg, PA: White Hat Communications, 2001.

Alan Bock — *Waiting to Inhale: The Politics of Medical Marijuana.* Santa Ana, CA: Seven Locks Press, 2000.

Tom Carnwath and Ian Smith — *Heroin Century.* New York: Routledge, 2002.

Rosalyn Carson-DeWitt, ed. — *Drugs, Alcohol, and Tobacco: Learning About Addictive Behavior.* New York: MacMillan Reference USA, 2003.

Rod Colvin — *Prescription Drug Addiction: The Hidden Epidemic.* Omaha, NE: Addicus Books, 2002.

Bruce Cotter — *When They Won't Quit: A Call to Action for Families, Friends, and Employers of Alcohol and Drug-Addicted People.* Hunt Valley, MD: Holly Hill, 2002.

Richard Davenport-Hines — *The Pursuit of Oblivion: A Global History of Narcotics.* New York: W.W. Norton, 2002.

James DeSena — *Overcoming Your Alcohol, Drug, and Recovery Habits: An Empowering Alternative to AA and 12-Step Treatment.* Tucson, AZ: See Sharp Press, 2003.

Robert L. Dupont and Betty Ford — *The Selfish Brain: Learning from Addiction.* Washington, DC: Hazelden Information Education, 2000.

Larry K. Gaines and Peter B. Kraska — *Drugs, Crime, and Justice.* Prospect Heights, IL: Waveland Press, 2003.

Avram Goldstein — *Addiction: From Biology to Drug Policy.* New York: Oxford University Press, 2001.

James P. Gray — *Why Our Drug Laws Have Failed and What We Can Do About It: A Judicial Indictment on the War on Drugs.* Philadelphia: Temple University Press, 2001.

Mike Gray, ed. — *Busted: Stone Cowboys, Narco-Lords, and Washington's War on Drugs.* New York: Thunder's Mouth Press/Nation Books, 2002.

Glen Hanson, Peter Venturelli, and Annette E. Fleckenstein, eds. — *Drugs and Society.* Boston: Jones and Bartlett, 2001.

Gene Hawes and Anderson Hawes	*Addiction Free: How to Help an Alcoholic or Addict Get Started on Recovery*. New York: Thomas Dunne, 2001.
Douglas Husak	*Legalize This: The Case for Decriminalizing Drugs*. New York: Verson, 2002.
Janet E. Joy, Stanley J. Watson Jr., and John A. Benson Jr., eds.	*Marijuana and Medicine: Assessing the Science Base*. Washington, DC: National Academy Press, 1999.
Timothy Lynch, ed.	*After Prohibition: An Adult Approach to Drug Policies in the 21st Century*. Washington, DC: Cato, 2000.
Robert J. MacCoun and Peter Reuter	*Drug War Heresies: Learning from Other Vices, Times, and Places*. New York: Cambridge University Press, 2001.
Alison Mack and Janet Joy	*Marijuana as Medicine: The Science Beyond the Controversy*. Washington, DC: National Academy Press, 2000.
Charles F. Manski, John V. Pepper, and Carol V. Petrie, eds.	*Informing America's Policy on Illegal Drugs: What We Don't Know Keeps Hurting Us*. Washington, DC: National Academy Press, 2001.
Bill McCollum, ed.	*Medical Marijuana Referenda Movement in America*. Washington, DC: Diane, 2001.
Barry Meier	*Pain Killer: A "Wonder" Drug's Trail of Addiction and Death*. Emmaus, PA: Rodale, 2003.
Brian Preston	*Pot Planet: Adventures in Global Marijuana Culture*. New York: Grove Atlantic, 2002.
Ed Rosenthal and Steve Kubby	*Why Marijuana Should Be Legal*. New York: Thunder's Mouth Press, 2003.
Joseph Santoro, Robert Deletis, and Alfred Bergman	*Kill the Craving: How to Control the Impulse to Use Drugs and Alcohol*. Oakland, CA: New Harbinger, 2001.
Jeffrey A. Schaler	*Addiction Is a Choice*. Peru, IL: Carus, 2000.
Dan Shapiro	*Mom's Marijuana*. New York: Vintage Books, 2001.
Lonny Shavelson	*Hooked: Five Addicts Challenge Our Misguided Rehab System*. New York: New Press, 2001.
Jacob Sullum	*Saying Yes: In Defense of Drug Use*. New York: J.P. Tarcher, 2003.
Samuel Walker	*Sense and Nonsense About Crime and Drugs: A Policy Guide*. Belmont, CA: Wadsworth, 2000.
Brett Alan Weinberg and Bonnie K. Bealer	*The World of Caffeine: The Science and Culture of the World's Most Popular Drug*. New York: Routledge, 2001.

Index